Secret Stories
of
Walt Disney
World

Other Books by Jim Korkis, from Theme Park Press:

The Vault of Walt: Volume 4 (2015)

The Everything I Know I Learned from Disney Animated Features (2015)

The Vault of Walt: Volume 3 (2014)

Animation Anecdotes (2014)

Who's the Leader of the Club? Walt Disney's Leadership Lessons (2014)

The Book of Mouse (2013)

The Vault of Walt: Volume 2 (2013)

Who's Afraid of the Song of the South? (2012)

The Revised Vault of Walt (2012)

Secret Stories of Walt Disney World

Things You Never Knew You Never Knew

Jim Korkis

Foreword by Sam Gennawey

Theme Park Press
www.ThemeParkPress.com

Editor: Bob McLain
Layout: Artisanal Text

ISBN 978-1-941500-68-2
Printed in the United States of America

Theme Park Press | **www.ThemeParkPress.com**
Address queries to bob@themeparkpress.com

Dedicated to Lonnie Hicks, a long-time cast member at Walt Disney World, whose passion for Disney history and finding out the true stories behind the stories has been inspirational. His friendship, good humor, and generosity have enriched my life and the lives of many others.

This book was written so he didn't have to keep referring to the voluminous collection of handwritten notes he painstakingly took at dozens of my presentations when I worked at Walt Disney World.

Contents

PART TWO:
THE WALT DISNEY WORLD RESORTS

Foreword

Jim Korkis. Kind of a legend for us Disney geeks. For example, sitting on my desk is a large stack of Disney related books written by the man.

The first thing that I notice is the number of Post-it notes that line the edge of the pages so I can find material on that page for future reference. There is a good reason for this. For years, Jim has been my go-to-guy for anything related to Disney. I've quoted him in my books. I can feel comfortable that the information is reliable and factual. After all, he created the job of Disney historian.

Jim has been a good friend for many years, and lately I sense that he is on a mission. He is the guy who first noticed that Disney historical knowledge is moving more toward myth and marketing than fact.

And he is here to stop that. Jim rightly believes that truth is stranger and more interesting than fiction and continues to prove he is right in all the stories he has produced over the years. I agree.

There are a lot of WDW trivia books out there, but this is a Jim Korkis WDW story book. Many of these stories are printed for the first time based on Jim's vast network of contacts including Disney executives, front line cast members, Reedy Creek officials, Imagineers, and others who worked at the parks for decades and had access to information that most people did not.

Ever the historian, Jim spent countless hours scouring the many different departmental libraries at Walt Disney World that were only available to members of that particular department. Some of those libraries like the ones for Feature Animation, Entertainment, and Disney University, no longer exist at all, so no one else will ever be able to use the resources Jim found there.

Because he wrote behind-the-scenes tours for guests and convention groups as part of one of his roles with Walt Disney World, Jim was given special permission to use those libraries to obtain the correct information, and we all benefit from what he discovered and now so generously shares.

All of this fact-finding is one thing. More importantly, Jim weaves together this knowledge in a way that does not destroy the magic, but enhances the understanding and appreciation of Walt Disney World. It certainly does so for me.

But this is nothing new. As I said before, Jim's research has become a central part of my Disney library, and I am sure that is the case for many of you as well. This book will be yet another welcome and valuable addition to my personal Disney collection.

Okay, so now that I have finished this foreword, I think it is time to pack my bags, hop on a plane, visit Walt Disney World, and see things through a new perspective, thanks to these eye-opening stories that were new to me and probably for the rest of you as well.

Many thanks, Jim.

Sam Gennawey

Sam Gennawey is an urban planner and author. He has penned *Walt Disney and the Promise of Progress City*, *The Disneyland Story: The Unofficial Guide to the Evolution of Walt Disney's Dream*, and *Universal vs. Disney: The Unofficial Guide to American Theme Parks Greatest Rivalry*. He is a frequent speaker at professional conferences, colleges and universities, and Disney history groups.

Introduction

"You should write a book!"

Whenever I am with friends and family visiting Walt Disney World, I can't help pointing out some of the interesting stories and details. Without fail, they usually ask if there is some sort of book that recounts this information, and I have to tell them that no such book exists.

Besides my own personal research and interest in Walt Disney World, I used to work there writing tours for guests, convention groups, internal cast member groups, and different departments as an instructor for Disney Adult Discoveries and Disney Institute. I not only facilitated those tours, but also trained others to give them.

I always had to make sure I had more information than what was shared during the tour in case someone had particular questions. I put together big binders with that additional information to help those who gave the tours. Once I was laid off five years ago, those binders disappeared almost immediately as having no value, despite them being filled with short interviews I had done with Imagineers and executives intimately connected to Walt Disney World.

I always went to primary sources, cross-checked the information with the Disney Archives and the multiple department libraries on property, and even then had to be constantly alert in case something changed.

I always hoped someone would indeed write a book about all the stories and details, because they were fascinating. I tried to actively encourage several others to do so with no success.

However, over the years, while there have been multiple books about Disneyland, most of the books that have appeared about Walt Disney World are usually trivia books.

Since most of these authors never worked at Walt Disney World nor had access to the information that I did, too often the material is out of date, misleading, incomplete, or outright false.

The same "secrets" seem to be cut-and-pasted to different books and websites over and over in the belief that since they appeared in print somewhere, they must be true.

At a high profile Disney event at the Contemporary Resort, I was served by a waiter who had worked at WDW for forty years. He confidently told me that Dick Nunis, the former chairman of Walt Disney Attractions, had told him that the primary reason Walt Disney built in Florida was that Walt once worked as a postman in Kissimmee.

That was not true, and I am sure that Dick Nunis never said anything to that effect. Walt's father, Elias, who lived briefly in the central Florida area during the late 1800s, held various jobs there, including hotel manager and rural postman on a buckboard in Kissimmee, but Walt himself never worked as a postman in Florida. Nunis may have been referring to Walt's father, if indeed he said anything at all.

It was obvious that the waiter had misheard or misremembered the information, and now shared it with great authority without verifying the facts. A little knowledge is often a very dangerous thing for Disney fans.

Walt had many reasons for choosing to build Walt Disney World in Orlando, from the weather to tourist patterns to inexpensive land. His dad's job as a postman in Kissimmee was not one of those reasons, nor was the fact that his parents got married in the area.

The waiter refused to be dissuaded by this information. He knew what he had heard and no one had ever corrected him. If anything, he had great pity for my ignorance and lack of common sense to accept the truth.

Just this last year, I was on a tour where a Magic Kingdom Guest Relations guide proudly pointed to the upper window of the train station to tell our group that it was there where Walt Disney used to sit to observe the park. After the tour, I privately pointed out that Walt had died in 1966 and that the Walt Disney World's train station had not opened until 1971.

Once again, the person just smiled condescendingly. Since currently I did not work at Walt Disney World, she thought I was just too stupid to know the real story. Of course, she didn't want to embarrass a guest by telling him that he was stupid, but felt that the information in the script she had been given must have been checked by higher-ups somewhere, and was true.

Walt Disney World cast members are constantly changing Disney history, and not necessarily for the better. Cast members at the Haunted Mansion created the names for the hitchhiking ghosts that seem to be accepted by everyone as canon. But Imagineer Marc Davis, who designed the ghosts, told me that they never had names, nor was there ever any intention to give them names beyond "hitchhiking ghosts".

WDW cast members also created the myth that Gracey is the master of the mansion. That isn't true, according to Imagineer X. Atencio who wrote the epitaphs on the tombstones in the grave-yard, including the one for "Master Gracey". Atencio told me that the tombstone was supposed to be an in-joke about the boyish nature of Imagineer Yale Gracey. "Master" was a term used for a young boy who was not old enough to be called "mister".

Cast members also insist on rearranging three of the plates on the table at the banquet so they form a "Hidden Mickey", despite Imagineers' constant efforts to change it back to the original configuration. Even though the Imagineers physically marked the table to indicate where the plates should go, the Hidden Mickey continually returns.

Other WDW cast members have fabricated stories that are told over and over to their peers and guests with an air of authority. Guests have been entertained by all sorts of falsehoods by bus drivers and accept the information as true because it is being shared by a cast member. Often these stories end up on Wikipedia or Google, which gives them an added sense of veracity to some people because they appear in print or on the internet.

So, I finally decided I should indeed write a book and get into print the *actual* stories, and have them available for people who want to verify what they've heard, with a reliable source.

These stories are only "secret" because they were often never told to the guests or even the cast members in most cases. That's one of the reasons some cast members made up their own versions to fill that unknown void.

This book contains just a small sample of the many stories about Walt Disney World. They are self-contained so can be read in any order, but that means there may be occasional repetition of some facts. There are several stories that relate to things that no longer exist, but might be of interest to long-time visitors who once experienced them or who enjoy history.

Everyone is entitled to their own opinion, but no one is entitled to make up their own facts, especially when they conflict with the actual facts. Preserving the truth about Walt Disney World has become a greater and greater challenge as the years pass, people who know the truth die or their memories start to get confused, and the Disney company does not aggressively share the real stories with cast members and guests.

Sometimes even the Disney company itself no longer knows the real stories. In the rush to complete a project on an impossible deadline, there was often no time to properly document the project or make any last-minute changes in a document if they occurred. As soon as one challenge was completed, it was immediately off to a new project.

The philosophy was always "we'll do that later", but "later" never came. I saw it happen many times on WDW projects in which I was involved.

This book is intended to be a foundation to help others do further research and to enrich their understanding of the most magical place on earth.

Please feel free to share these true stories with your friends and family. Everyone will think you are the Disney expert, and not one of them will ask if you heard the story from Jim Korkis, but they may ask if you checked it first with a WDW bus driver, waiter, or tour guide who had told them something quite different.

Jim Korkis
Disney Historian
October 2015

The Birth of Walt Disney World

Walt Disney World consists of four distinct theme parks, twenty-eight hotel resorts owned by Disney, two water parks, a shopping district, five golf courses, and much, much more.

As soon as Disneyland opened in 1955, Walt Disney realized that he needed more space for expansion and to enable him to control the area around the park that had filled up with cheap motels, tacky shops, and ugly billboards.

It irritated Walt that guests had to drive through this congestion of chaos and cheapness to get to and from his magic kingdom. He did not have enough money to buy the surrounding land when building the park, and by the time he did, real estate prices around Disneyland had soared astronomically.

Surveys showed that roughly two-thirds of the visitors to Disneyland came from the California area. Less than eight percent of the guests came from east of the Mississippi, even though that's where almost seventy-five percent of Americans lived.

Walt decided that if he bought more land it should be somewhere on the East Coast to tap into that potential audience. He needed enough land to hold all of his dreams and he looked at many different locations around the country, including St. Louis, Missouri; southern Florida; and Niagara Falls.

By November 1963, Walt had finally settled on a large section of land in central Florida. That decision began a secret operation to purchase the land before prices skyrocketed once it was discovered that Disney was interested. Eventually, the company was able to purchase forty-three square miles of land before it was officially revealed that Disney was the buyer.

Central Florida was picked for several reasons. The location is up the coast and inland, so it is not near the beach or hurricane activity.

The weather would permit year-round operation, unlike some other East Coast locations. It was at the intersection of two major highways (north/south and east/west) capturing traffic going both ways across the state. Large chunks of land could be bought inexpensively.

It was reasoned that people driving down to Miami for vacation would stop at Walt Disney World or stop there on their way back home. Amusingly, once Walt Disney World opened, visitors did not continue on down to Miami, but were content to make Walt Disney World their sole destination.

Walt always claimed he would never build another Disneyland. His plans for the property included the building of an experimental community that would also include some type of an entertainment venue, because that is what people wanted. That entertainment venue was to be similar in spirit to Disneyland, but much different in content. The plan was to have an East Coast turn-of-the-century theme for Main Street, U.S.A., and different attractions than those at Disneyland, including ones based on the movies *Mary Poppins*, *Sword in the Stone*, and *The Legend of Sleepy Hollow*.

When Walt passed away in December 1966, his older brother Roy took charge and changed the name of the project from "Disney World" to "Walt Disney World" so that people would remember it was his brother's idea.

Roy realized that financially it made more sense to build the entertainment venue first to generate income to pay for the experimental community. In addition, it was less expensive to include some of the familiar rides from Disneyland mixed in with new attractions like the Mickey Mouse Revue and the Country Bear Jamboree. It was also assumed that East Coast guests were eager to ride these attractions that they had seen on television, but that they might never ride without making the long trip to Disneyland.

Jack Lindquist, Director of Marketing for Walt Disney World in 1971, said:

> Without Roy, [Walt Disney World] wouldn't have happened. Everyone else was so in awe of Walt that they could not step forward and take his place. It took a Disney to do it and that was Roy.

Roy O. Disney was 73 years old and planning to retire when he stepped in and he decided, against the recommendations of others at the Disney Company, to build Walt's final dream the way Walt intended.

Aware of his own limitations, Roy put Richard Irvine, the president of WED (Imagineering) in charge of creative development, and Admiral Joe Fowler in charge of construction. (General Joe Potter prepared the land for construction.)

Many other talented people were responsible for the design and construction of WDW, but the two Magic Kingdom steamboats were named the *Richard F. Irvine* and the *Admiral Joe Fowler* to acknowledge the right and left hand of Roy O. Disney in making Walt's dream a reality.

Walt Disney World was to be a complete vacation destination, so the plan included the building of hotel resorts and activities ranging from water sports to golfing to horseback riding and more.

However, fearing a repeat of the turmoil of Disneyland's disastrous opening in 1955, the Disney Company proclaimed that the entire month of October 1971 was the "preview month" for the Magic Kingdom and hoped that after three weeks of operation, everything would be running smoothly in time for the official dedication a week before Halloween.

Two days before the opening of Walt Disney World on October 1, 1971, the Florida Highway Patrol issued a statement that they had determined that as many as 300,000 people might try to be among the first to get into the Magic Kingdom on that first day.

Actually, the first of October had been selected by the Disney Company as the slowest day of the week in Orlando's slowest month of the year to try to keep crowds manageable, fearing a repeat of the disastrous opening of Disneyland in 1955 where many more people than expected flooded into the park and there were challenges with food and attractions.

The night before opening, workers were still either instituting temporary measures where the job could not be completed by the next morning or making final finishing touches. It had been the largest privately funded construction project in the world. More than nine thousand workers labored over two years to have it ready on October 1st at a cost of more than $400 million.

Guests had already started lining up at the toll booths by midnight, so some workers slept overnight in the Magic Kingdom for fear they might not be able to get back the next morning because of the traffic.

When the Magic Kingdom officially opened at 10 a.m., Jack Lindquist had already picked the first family to enter the new Disney theme park. That lucky sandy-haired father was William "Bill" Windsor Jr. from nearby Lakeland, Florida, who was accompanied by his pretty blue-eyed wife, Marty, and their sons Jay (age three) and Lee (just under nineteen months). The family had arrived so early that they had slept in their car overnight at the nearest roadside rest area in order to be among the first into the parking lot.

As expected by the Disney Company, roughly ten thousand guests showed up and everything went smoothly. Roy O. Disney was enraged at the reaction on Wall Street and in the media that the Disney Company had underperformed on its first opening day. Disney stock prices immediately dropped because of the feeling that Disney had made a fatal misstep.

Card Walker, at the time a Disney executive vice president and its chief operating officer, said later:

> The worst time in my life was at the Polynesian on opening day, a question-and-answer session with newsmen. They were asking why there were only 10,000 people that day. All of us wanted to kill ourselves.

Three weeks later, over 40,000 guests jammed the Magic Kingdom on Saturday October 23, 1971, for the beginning of the official three-day dedication of Walt Disney World. Those three days included a special performance by the World Symphony Orchestra, the filming of a television special, banquets like a special beach luau at the Polynesian featuring the debut of the Electrical Water Pageant, and famed composer Meredith Wilson conducting a 1,076 piece marching band on Main Street.

For many, the highlight was Roy O. Disney's memorable reading of the dedication plaque that would be enshrined on the ground near the Town Square flagpole on Main Street, U.S.A. It was unique because it was not just a dedication of the Magic Kingdom park, but all of Walt Disney World:

> Walt Disney World is a tribute to the philosophy and life of Walter Elias Disney...and to the talents, the dedication, and the loyalty of the entire Disney organization that made Walt Disney's dream come true. May Walt Disney World bring joy and inspiration and new knowledge to all who come to this happy place...a Magic Kingdom where the young at heart of all ages can laugh and play and learn—together. Dedicated this 25th day of October, 1971. Roy O. Disney.

As Disney publicist Charlie Ridgway remembered it

Having forecast (internally) a first-year guest count of eight million, Walt's brother Roy told associates, 'Unless we have a full house for Thanksgiving weekend, we're in trouble.' Turkey day brought a crunch of first-time visitors jamming roads in every direction. With only 5,000 hotel rooms in the area plus fifteen hundred in Disney's two hotels, eager fans were camped out along the Florida Turnpike and 1-75 all the way to the Georgia border, about two hundred miles away.

The Friday and Saturday after Thanksgiving Thursday was dubbed "The Traffic Jam Heard 'Round the World".

The Magic Kingdom quickly reached its capacity of roughly 50,000 guests early in the day, with over 5000 cars being turned away from the parking lot. The traffic congestion on Interstate 4 leading into Walt Disney World was backed up for over twenty miles. One news report declared it "the longest parking lot in the world". Ridgway said:

> Christmas week was even busier. Our fifteen hundred rooms in the Contemporary and the Polynesian were booked up for a year.

Officially during that first year, the Magic Kingdom attracted 10,712,991 guests (most articles rounded it up to an even 11,000,000) and recorded total gross revenues amounting to $139 million. Walt Disney World property had been assessed for tax purposes at about $150 million with a tax bill that would run about $3 million and another $9 million generated in sales taxes.

Sales at local area restaurants, lunch rooms, and catering services increased 94%. Even candy sales at stores surrounding Walt Disney World were up 18%.

Hotels and motels were booked solid with tourists being diverted to Tampa and Daytona Beach for lodging (and an additional hour's drive back to Walt Disney World). Before the theme park opened, the Orlando area offered about 5,800 hotel and motel rooms. By June 1972, the total had jumped to about 10,000 rooms, with another 7,000 rooms under construction.

Orlando realtor Jack Gale reported that land adjoining Disney on the north "is a good buy at $3,750 an acre", but pointed out "up to $120,000 per acre has been paid for some high-density development land in the immediate area". (The Disney Company had paid on average about $182 an acre, which was considered a generous price for swamp land.)

Citrus growers often awoke early in the morning to find people in their groves either wanting to buy fresh oranges or to buy the land itself.

In 1967, Orange County showed 68,005 acres in citrus trees. By 1972, that figure, according to the most recent survey, had fallen to 60,551 acres, and was continuing to drop. The same decline in citrus groves was seen in Seminole County and Osceola County, as farmers simply could not afford to turn down the prices being offered for their land.

The Orlando branch of the Salvation Army that helped 18,000 indigent transients in 1966 recorded 67,000 cases in 1971. The ever-increasing numbers were putting considerable strain on their facilities and supplies. Director Richard Bergren stated that the Salvation Army in 1972 had gone $19,000 in debt feeding transient indigents who had come to town with no money and no jobs, but simply hope of finding work.

While the largest employer in the area was Walt Disney World, official spokesmen emphasized that Disney was only seeking employees in the central Florida area "between 20 and 25 years old for guide-type jobs", and of course, costumes were only made in certain sizes (not the wide variety available today) that favored the more slender applicant.

The work force at Walt Disney World in early 1972 was 10,400, but was expected to swell to 12,100 for the upcoming summer months. The Magic Kingdom's weekly payroll was documented as $1.1 million per week.

In its April 8, 1972, issue, *The Saturday Review* described Disney World cast members as:

> [F]resh faced kids who run the part of the enterprise already under sail look as if they were recruited from the national company of Up With People. They are unfailingly pleasant, unfailingly neat, properly—if that's today correct word—coifed or barbered, and taken all together, are what one's grandmother would call "nice looking boys and girls".

Overall in Orlando, employment was up more than eleven percent in April 1972 compared with April 1971. and unemployment was a low 2.8 percent.

Like countless other publications, *Architectural Forum* (June 1972) also extolled the positive environmental philosophy on the Disney property:

> WDW is the first New Town in the U.S. to set aside almost one third of its total acreage to a spectacular conservation project—7,500 acres of Everglades-type jungle, inhabited by alligators, birds, snakes, bears, fish, and exotic trees, and forever protected from vandals.

The opening of Walt Disney World had an impact on the surrounding attractions as well. Cypress Gardens reported that, by June 1972, business had increased 38%, with expectations for the summer months to be "something that Florida will long remember".

Cape Kennedy stated that visitors taking tours of its space facility increased more than 27% in just the first four months of 1972. During that same period, St. Augustine recorded a 29% increase in visitors. Even Silver Springs, with its gentle glass-bottomed boat tour, saw an increase of visitors of 28% within the first quarter of 1972.

Interestingly, while Disney expected that after visiting the theme park tourists would travel down to southern Florida, it didn't work out that way. Miami was hurt the most, with only 6.9% of tourists saying their destination was Miami, whereas the months before Walt Disney World opened it had been 9.8%, and forecast to climb even higher.

Increased tourism (and the resulting increased sales taxes) resulted in the general revenue fund for Florida to show a surplus of $207 million by the beginning of summer 1972. The legislature used almost $100 million dollars of that money on long-delayed building programs and still had a $50 million working surplus fund.

Of course, all of the expansion also brought an increased crime rate, including drugs. Only four drug arrests had been made in the Orlando area during the entire year of 1966, but in the beginning months of 1972, there had already been 256 such arrests. Other crimes that increased dramatically ranged from theft to prostitution. In addition, there were also increased property taxes and traffic challenges.

However, Disney spokesmen pointed out that those negative aspects were more a reflection of the changing times than the presence of Disney in Florida.

In truth, the opening of Walt Disney World could not be directly blamed for the increased ills plaguing Orlando. The Disney Company was highly diligent in screening and monitoring all its employees. However, the Disney-inspired prosperity did attract a criminal element and a variety of social misfits who, as in the California Gold Rush of 1949, flooded into the area looking for quick riches.

In 1972, the daily traffic count at an Interstate 4 location between Gore Avenue and Anderson Street showed a 34% increase, with roughly 82,460 cars whizzing by that stretch every twenty-four hours. The first six months of 1972 clocked a nearly 23% increase in the use of the Florida Turnpike, with toll revenues close to $30 million. While Eastern Airlines, the official airline of Walt Disney World, doubled its flights to Orlando from 40 to 80 at the beginning of 1972, nearly 80% of tourists still arrived to Florida in an automobile.

At the first anniversary of the opening of Walt Disney World, Robert Jackson, the director of the Office of Information Services, United States Travel Service, U.S. Department of Commerce stated:

> Early in its first year, Walt Disney World moved to Position Number One on the list of United States destinations of greatest interest to the international travel industry... WDW has been significantly responsible for the increased vacation plans by the international tourist... WDW has also played a very important role as a strong counter-balance to the negative sociological influences that have often injured the nation's image abroad... With only a year's history behind it, Walt Disney World has already had an extraordinary past.

That first Year of the Mouse had been a busy and prosperous one. With new additions planned for the next few years, it seemed like it would be a great big beautiful tomorrow.

Disney Chairman of the Board Donn Tatum wrote in Disney's 1972 Annual Report:

> It is the year which saw us bring on stream, on a fully operative basis, Walt Disney World, a project the scope and complexity of which are difficult to describe—let alone comprehend—and the future of which will undoubtedly add more great chapters to our Company's history.

During the next forty-five years, Walt Disney World did expand more than even Walt himself could have dreamed. It is such an overwhelming, spectacular experience that guests sometimes forget to take a minute to fully enjoy some of the wonderful individual elements, and the stories behind those things.

On the following pages are some insights into a few of those secret stories. There are many more secret stories left to tell.

PART ONE

The Walt Disney World Parks

The Themed Entertainment Association compiled attendance data for the year 2014 which included the fact that, in total, 148,341,000 people attended theme parks globally during that year. Here are the top twenty theme parks in the world, ranked by attendance:

1. Magic Kingdom (WDW): 19,332,000
2. Tokyo Disneyland: 17,300,000
3. Disneyland (Anaheim, California): 16,769,000
4. Tokyo Disney Sea: 14,100,000
5. Universal Studios Japan: 11,800,000
6. Epcot (WDW): 11,454,000
7. Disney's Animal Kingdom (WDW): 10,402,000
8. Disney Hollywood Studios (WDW): 10,312,000
9. Disneyland Paris: 9,940,000
10. Disneyland California Adventure Park: 8,769,000
11. Universal Studios (Universal Orlando): 8,263,000
12. Islands of Adventure (Universal Orlando): 8,141,000
13. Ocean Park (Hong Kong): 7,792,000
14. Lotte World (Seoul, South Korea): 7,606,000
15. Hong Kong Disneyland: 7,500,000
16. Everland (Gyeonggi-Do, South Korea): 7,381,000
17. Universal Studios Hollywood: 6,824,000
18. Songcheng Park (Hangzhou, China): 5,810,000
19. Nagashima Spa Land (Kuwana, Japan): 5,630,000
20. Chimelong Ocean Kingdom (Hengqin, China): 5,504,000

Cinderella Castle

Cinderella Castle opened October 1, 1971, as the symbol for the entire Walt Disney World Resort. It is 189 feet high. It took approximately eighteen months to build, and was completed in July 1971.

The castle is made of concrete, steel, cement, gypsum plaster, plastic shingles, and fiberglass over a 600-ton framework of steel. No bricks were used in the construction. At the time it was first built, it was the largest fiberglass structure in the world.

Large stone shapes are used at the bottom, then the stones get progressively smaller toward the top of the structure, which helps give the impression that the castle is taller than it actually is.

The design took the form of a romanticized composite of such fabled French courts as Fontainebleau, Versailles, and a dozen chateaux of the Loire Valley, including Chenonceau, Chambord and Chaumont.

The emphasis on French architecture was because the Disney animated feature film *Cinderella* (1950) was based on French writer Charles Perrault's popular version of the fairy tale, and not the one from the Brothers Grimm. In addition, there is the influence of the blue-tipped turrets of the Alcazar in Segovia, Spain.

The columns that are in the walkway of Cinderella Castle are decorated with mice and birds from the Disney film. (The female mice are named Suzy and Perla.) These characters were sculpted by Blaine Gibson, who also sculpted the Cinderella Wishing Well statue located just outside the castle.

The story of Cinderella is displayed on five glittering mosaic murals in the walkway of the castle, with each decorated panel in the shape of a Gothic arch, 15-feet high and 10-feet wide. The mosaic was designed by Disney artist Dorothea Redmond, and crafted by a team of six people who took approximately two years to completely install the murals under the supervision of renowned mosaicist Hanns-Joachim Scharff.

The five murals contain hundreds of thousands of pieces of glass, many of them fused with silver and 14-carat gold. More than 500 colors were used to create the murals. Cinderella's stepsisters, Drizella and Anastasia, are "red"-faced with anger and "green"-faced with envy.

The bearded royal courtier is a caricature of Imagineer John Hench and the other is Imagineer Herb Ryman, who designed both Sleeping Beauty Castle in Disneyland and Cinderella Castle in Walt Disney World.

One Disney "urban myth" is that in the event of a hurricane, the castle can be dismantled. That is untrue. The main building has an internal grid of steel framing, secured to a concrete foundation. The turrets and towers also have internal steel framing and were lifted by crane, then bolted permanently to the main structure.

Since people saw the castle being assembled in two separate sections, they assumed it could be dismantled that way as well. The castle can withstand hurricane winds of at least 90 miles per hour.

With the passing of Roy Disney in 1971, it was decided not to complete the small suite designed by Dorothea Redmond inside Cinderella Castle that would have served as an apartment for the Disney family.

Instead, over the years, the area was used as the operations unit for switchboard operators, storage, and finally, a dressing room for the entertainers performing in the shows at the Castle Forecourt Stage.

In 2005, the Walt Disney Company decided to use the location as it was originally intended, as a private suite, transforming it into a royal bed chamber called Cinderella's Castle Suite for use in special promotions and by specially chosen guests.

Prince Charming Regal Carousel

The Walt Disney World Carousel in the Magic Kingdom was built in 1917 by the Philadelphia Toboggan Company, which created some of the most beautiful horses of the era.

It was carved by German and Italian carvers to express the patriotism that was prevalent in the United States after World War I. The carousel was named "Liberty", and was one of the largest carousels ever built, being some sixty feet in diameter.

The first home of the Liberty Carousel was at the Detroit Palace Garden Park where it stayed until it was rehabilitated in Philadelphia in 1928 and set up in Olympic Park in Maplewood, N.J., for the next 39 years.

The carousel originally had 72 horses and two chariots (not four as is reported in some articles). The distinctly American horses were black, brown, gray, and white.

Their saddles included items that celebrated the American frontier. Carved figures of Lady Liberty holding shields that featured a red, white, and blue flag emblem decorated the interior top circle.

There were eighteen landscape paintings of American scenery. Just below was a running board decorated with golden American eagles. Over the years, less skilled craftsmen would slop paint and lacquer over the horses, eventually obscuring the intricate and uniquely engraved features underneath.

The Philadelphia Toboggan Company only built 89 carousels before 1929 and the Great Depression. The Liberty Carousel is No. 46 and one of only a dozen or less of those classic originals from that company which still exist and operate today.

Olympic Park closed in 1965. By that point, the Liberty Carousel had fallen into a state of disrepair and was slated for almost-certain demolition. Antique carousel horses are in such demand that it was planned to sell them and the decorations off individually.

By 1967, however, Disney had located and acquired this antique masterpiece for the Magic Kingdom.

All of the horses were shipped to Disney Central Shops, where craftsmen were surprised by the detail and artistic grace uncovered when all the layers of paint and grime were removed down to the gleaming maplewood of the horses. Months of Disney artistry went into their rehabilitation.

The chariots were removed and the carousel was filled out to 90 horses when Disney purchased some antique horses made by two other well-known producers of carousels: the Dentzel Company and the Parker Company.

The horses were sanded down carefully to the original wood so that no detail was lost. Sanding down to the actual wood could have resulted in damage and loss of detail, so, today, they are only sanded down to roughly the level of primer, and no further. Then the horses were primed and painted white.

The horses are white for two reasons. First, since it was Cinderella's carousel, the white horses reference the white horses that pulled Cinderella's pumpkin coach. Second, one of the things Disney discovered with King Arthur's Carrousel at Disneyland was that when people rode a carousel, they first tried to get on a white horse because it was considered the "hero" horse.

It was Imagineer John Hench who made the decision to make all the horses at Disneyland and Walt Disney World arctic white. Every guest, no matter their size or speed, gets a chance to ride a "hero" horse.

In 1997, one of the original chariots was located in a Disney warehouse and rehabbed and reinstalled on the ride. For decades, the attraction was named Cinderella's Golden Carousel, but was renamed Prince Charming Regal Carousel in 2010.

Partners Statue

In 1962, Blaine Gibson (who would later be renowned for his sculpting skills in Disney theme park attractions like Pirates of the Caribbean and Hall of Presidents) sculpted a bust of Walt as a "thank you" gift.

Gibson claimed that when he presented it, Walt said, "What am I going to do with this? Statues are for dead people."

He later used it as reference for a bust of Walt at the Academy of Television Arts & Science (ATAS) headquarters in North Hollywood, California, when Walt was inducted in 1986. A duplicate casting of that bust is also at Disney's Hollywood Studios in the ATAS Hall of Fame Plaza next to the Hyperion Theater.

Imagineers Marty Sklar and John Hench were particularly concerned that in the two decades since Walt's death, he was being forgotten by new generations who had not seen him on television each week. They felt there needed to be a significant reminder in the park.

Of course, with all his experience, Gibson was a natural choice to sculpt the statue, even though he had retired from the company. Gibson made several different sketches, including one with Walt holding the rolled-up blueprints of Epcot in his hand and pointing forward. He explained:

> I chose to depict Walt as he was in 1954. I think that was when Walt was in his prime. It was tough trying to match the media image of Walt Disney, the one the public knows, to the real Walt, the one we knew. I think Walt is admiring the park and saying to Mickey, "Look what we've accomplished together," because truly they were very much a team through it all. "Look at all the happy people who have come to visit us today."

Gibson made the figure of Walt larger than life, roughly 6-feet, 5-inches tall. In real life, Walt was barely 5-feet, 10-inches tall. Gibson paid close attention to detail. The "STR" logo on Walt's tie refers to the Smoke Tree Ranch vacation area in Palm Springs where Walt had a home. The logo was on some of the ties that Walt would wear.

On Walt's right hand, in addition to the regular wedding ring that was on his left hand, is the Irish Claddagh wedding ring that he and his wife wore. Walt bought the pair in 1948 on a trip to Ireland where his ancestors once lived.

The size of Mickey Mouse was chosen based on a brief moment from the animated short, *The Pointer* (1939). Animator Frank Thomas recalled:

> When he recorded the voice, [Walt] couldn't help but feel like Mickey and he added all these little gestures that were spontaneous with him. At one point, he put out his hand like this [to indicate that Mickey was about 3 feet tall]; it was the only time we knew how big Walt thought Mickey was.

Marty Sklar remembers being amazed seeing Gibson and Hench spending hours discussing just exactly how Walt's five-fingered hand should hold Mickey's four-fingered one. It was finally decided to base it on the one time that an animated Mickey held the hand of a real person.

In *Fantasia* (1940), Mickey shakes the hand of conductor Leopold Stokowski.

The Walt Disney World *Partners* statue was unveiled in Florida in June 1995 with a plaque that states:

> We believe in our idea: a family park where parents and children could have fun—together—Walt Disney.

Roy O. Disney's
Sharing the Magic Statue

Imagineer Blaine Gibson began his Disney career in 1939 as an apprentice animation artist. Walt Disney noticed Gibson's interest and skill in sculpture and transferred him over to WED (Imagineering) to work on things for Disneyland.

Gibson ended up sculpting everything, including Indians along the banks of the Rivers of America, mermaids in the Submarine Voyage lagoon, bathing elephants on the Jungle Cruise, President Lincoln (as well as all the presidents in the Hall of Presidents except for President Obama, who was done by a Gibson protege), Haunted Mansion ghosts, and blood-thirsty pirates in Pirates of the Caribbean.

Gibson became a Disney Legend in 1993, the same year the *Partners* statue that he had sculpted was installed at Disneyland.

While Mickey truly was Walt's partner, Walt also had a "silent partner" who once said, "My younger brother dreams of castles, but I am the one that has to get them built."

A statue of Walt's older brother Roy O. Disney seated on a park bench beside Minnie Mouse at the Magic Kingdom theme park in Florida is located approximately where Roy stood when he dedicated the park in October 1971. This statue was installed in October 1999 and was also the work of Blaine Gibson.

The statue of Roy is called *Sharing the Magic* and sits by the flagpole in Town Square across the street from the confectionery shop where the upper window has Roy's name with the inscription: "If We Can Dream It—We Can Do It!"—Dreamers & Doers—Roy O. Disney, Chairman.

"Roy is sitting back in the bench which indicates he was there first and Minnie came to him, not that he came up to her to ask why she was sitting down and not working," laughed Gibson, who based the pose on photographs taken of Roy in the park in October 1971 sitting on a bench with a costumed Mickey Mouse. "Also, he is holding her hand underneath so he is supporting it, just like he always supported Walt's dreams. Roy was very underrated."

Originally, the statue was put behind a low fence, but so many guests climbed over the fence for photographs that it was moved into a public area.

Roy told reporters:

> Walt had this idea [for Walt Disney World]. My job all along was to help Walt do the things he wanted to do. He did the dreaming. I did the building.

A duplicate of the statue is located outside the Team Disney building at Disney's corporate headquarters in Burbank, California. There is a third statue at the Tokyo Disneyland theme park.

Disney marketing executive Jack Lindquist told author Bob Thomas:

> Without Roy, [Walt Disney World] wouldn't have happened. Everyone else was so in awe of Walt that they could not step forward and take his place. It took a Disney to do it and that was Roy.

Both the *Partners* and the *Sharing the Magic* statues are favorite photo locations at the Magic Kingdom today as they continue to honor the two brothers who made a dream come true in a Florida swampland.

Gibson's young assistant on both these statues was the very talented Rick Terry, the sculptor of the recent *Storytellers* statue of Walt and Mickey at Disney California Adventure.

Gibson looked over his shoulder, as did Imagineer Ray Spencer, while Terry worked on this newest icon in the Disney theme parks.

Tony's Town Square Restaurant

When Main Street, U.S.A. opened at the Magic Kingdom in October 1971, right there in Town Square was the Town Square Café with an open-air porch where patrons could watch the stream of guests rushing in and out of the park.

The food-and-beverage location offered breakfast, lunch, and dinner, and was themed to the elegant Victorian era. Originally, the venue was going to be sponsored by a coffee company, but the proposed participant backed out.

It ended up being sponsored by Oscar Mayer from 1971–1981. Little Oscar (affable George Molchan), the diminutive spokesman for the company, in his white chef's hat, was there greeting guests and handing out the iconic wiener whistles to eager children.

However, it was not Oscar Mayer hot dogs that were served at the location, but upscale fare like Monte Cristo sandwiches and Crepes Jambalaya. Both Coca-Cola and Pepsi-Cola were also available.

When Oscar Mayer declined to renew its sponsorship, the location was taken over by Hormel which handled the operation from 1981–1989. The menu was a large four-page newspaper entitled *Town Square Times* with the first page devoted to the history of the Hormel company. The new sponsor still sold a Monte Cristo sandwich along with a Main Street Deli Plate and fresh catfish.

When Hormel decided not to continue sponsorship in 1989, the Disney Company did an extensive renovation of the location, converting it into Tony's Town Square. It references the Italian restaurant in the Disney's animated film *Lady and the Tramp* (1955), where two canines shared a romantic moment over a plate of spaghetti and meat balls.

The proprietor of the film's eatery is a larger-than-life, black-mustached, friendly character named Tony, voiced by actor George Givot who was known for his dialect comedy and fine singing voice.

The waiting area has a television playing a clip from the film and the interior is decorated with *Lady and the Tramp*-inspired artwork as well as a sculpted fountain featuring the two characters.

For over thirty years, Don "Ducky" Williams has been a senior character artist at Walt Disney World. During that time, he supplied artwork for memorable pieces of merchandise and special projects. He told me:

> I did the artwork for all the china, signage, menus, etc. In fact, when it first opened, it had plates, saucers, creamers, and more with my *Lady and the Tramp* artwork on it. They found the guests loved it so much that they kept stealing it, so they replaced them with regular china. The remainder they had they sold at Disneyana conventions.
>
> Do you see all those framed paintings on the wall? There are twelve of them and I did them all. Those are the original paintings framed under glass, not prints or reproductions. If they ever change out that place, I would love to have those back to put up in my house.

In front of the restaurant, on the side walk, just like in the movie, someone outlined a heart when the cement was wet and there are two sets of dog paws. To the left of the restaurant is a sign for the Chapeau shop that features a hat box exactly like the one that little Lady was in at the beginning of the film. Details like these enhance the overall experience for sharp-eyed guests.

The Summer Magic Connections

While most Disney fans know that Main Street, U.S.A. is set during the time period of 1890–1910, few know that Walt Disney World's Main Street also pays special tribute to one of Walt Disney's favorite live-action movies, *Summer Magic*, first released on July 1963.

In the film, Boston widow Margaret Carey moves her family of two young sons and an exuberant teenage daughter, Nancy, to a house in Beulah, Maine, after the death of her husband. Her daughter (played by Hayley Mills) has written to Osh Popham (played by Burl Ives), the caretaker of an absent millionaire's abandoned big yellow house.

The headstrong and imaginative daughter writes such an exaggerated tale of heartbreaking white lies that Osh lets the family rent the house for a pittance and contributes labor and material to refurbish it.

While the family is happily settling in to their new life that summer in a rural East Coast community, their snobbish cousin Julia (who loves all things French) shows up to stay and causes anxiety for Nancy. Eventually, Julia learns the error of her snooty ways.

The film is a sentimental snapshot of a time period and a rural lifestyle that Walt Disney remembered fondly.

While no Burl Ives Streetmosphere performer sits rocking away on a nearby porch, strumming his guitar, his character in the film has a prominent location on Main Street.

In the lower part of one of the front windows of the Emporium, at the southwest corner entrance facing the Roy Disney statue by the flagpole, the name "Osh Popham" is listed as the proprietor of the store.

Osh was the shopkeeper, constable, carpenter, postmaster, and good-natured storyteller of the small town of Beulah, Maine.

The Chapeau, the hat shop in Town Square, is supposedly owned and operated by the two Carey girls. The sign outside lists its street address as "No. 63", the year the film was released.

According to the official back story created by WDW Imagineers:

> Nancy [Carey] moved to Main Street after spending many happy years with her family in the "yellow house" in beautiful Beulah. She had set out to seek her fortune, but she wanted to do something artistic, something that would bring happiness to people.
>
> And at the height of ragtime and hometown Easter parades, nothing could compare to fine headwear! So Nancy enlisted her notoriously fashion-conscious cousin, Julia Carey, and opened a small millinery and hat shop, where together they would design, make, and sell hats of all sorts for the ladies and gentlemen of Main Street. They dubbed their new venture the Chapeau, a suitably highbrow name reflecting the time Julia spent in the fashion capital of the world, Paris.

From 1992–2012, the background music loop for WDW's Main Street featured three instrumental versions of songs written by the legendary Sherman Brothers for the film: "Flitterin'", "Beautiful Beulah", and the title tune, "Summer Magic".

Most guests never realized that these sprightly tunes were not authentic turn-of-the-century songs, just as most guests are unaware of these other tributes in the park to a classic Disney live-action film.

Beacon Joe

Which original Disney character appears in three different attractions at Walt Disney World and was originally created for Disneyland?

The answer is in the title: Beacon Joe.

For many Disney fans, however, that is a puzzling answer.

When the Pirates of the Caribbean opened in May 1967, it was the last Disney attraction personally overseen by Walt Disney himself.

The always innovative Walt conceived of a quiet, upscale restaurant, to be called Blue Bayou, that would actually be inside Pirates of the Caribbean. It was an idea that had never been done before, and it was an instant hit with the many visitors to Disneyland.

There were discussions of including live entertainment in this quiet, restful environment, but after a dress rehearsal during a trial dinner, Walt reportedly said:

> In this restaurant, the food is going to be the show, along with the atmosphere.

In Pirates, right across from the Blue Bayou restaurant and to the left of the guests in the boats, is a shack where a bearded man wearing overalls leisurely rocks back and forth plucking out a tune on his banjo. That's Beacon Joe.

Disney artist/animator Marc Davis designed both the character and the shack. In fact, the initial concept drawing of the shack and the character came from Davis' original designs for a Thieves Market that was going to be part of Pirates of the Caribbean when it was planned to be a walk-through experience.

At first, Pirates was not going to be installed in Florida, and so to enhance the steamboat voyage around the Rivers of America in Frontierland, Davis situated Beacon Joe and his shack just around an upper curve in the river.

Joe was not there at the opening in 1971 but made his appearance sometime in late 1972 just before the opening of Tom Sawyer's Island in 1973 along with other residents added to the river banks like the Native Americans in their village.

Joe is the last outpost of civilization before guests drift into the frontier wilderness.

He sits on the porch of his shack in front of Alligator Swamp smoking his corncob pipe. He keeps track of the river's occasional course changes and marks the river accordingly for the river traffic.

His faithful dog intensely watches a jumping fish (that looks suspiciously like a repainted piranha from the Jungle Cruise) with his head turning from left to right.

Beacon Joe also appears in Tokyo Disneyland. He can be seen fishing, surrounded by barrels and with his faithful dog on the nearby stairs, near the large trestle of the Western River Railroad as the steamboat maneuvers around the Western River.

It is not unusual for the Disney company to re-use Audio-Animatronics sculpted figures. For instance, President Thomas Jefferson shows up as a sheriff on a balcony in the Great Movie Ride, along with some Caribbean pirates re-used as gangsters earlier in the attraction.

The character sculpt of Beacon Joe is used in Pirates of the Caribbean for the standing pirate in the last jail cell at the end of the ride trying to coax a dog to give him the key to the door. He also shows up clean-shaven and wearing a crown at the ballroom banquet table in the Haunted Mansion.

Just like a supporting character actor in a film, Beacon Joe quietly makes his appearances to help the storytelling, but never feels the necessity to be the star of the show.

Splash Mountain

Splash Mountain is loosely based on some of the incidents in the animated sections of the still controversial Disney live-action film *Song of the South* (1946). Br'er Rabbit runs away from home and finds himself in more adventures than he intended.

He continually outwits Br'er Fox and Br'er Bear until he is trapped in honey (rather than the politically incorrect Tar Baby in the movie) and taken to Br'er Fox's lair to be eaten.

As in the movie, he convinces Br'er Fox to toss him into the spiky Briar Patch where the plucky rabbit survives because he was born and bred in it, and knows how to escape.

The grand finale of that water flume drop into the briar patch has the Oscar-winning "Zip a Dee Doo Dah" song being sung by critters on a massive rocking showboat as Br'er Rabbit re-discovers the comforts of the home he tried to abandon.

Splash Mountain opened at Disneyland on July 17, 1989, and three years later, on July 17, 1992, at Walt Disney World's Magic Kingdom.

Officially, the attraction was dedicated at Magic Kingdom on October 2, 1992, but was up and running as a "soft open" for over two months during that summer, beginning July 17.

The two versions share many similarities and a handful of differences.

At Walt Disney World, the project was supervised by Imagineer Eric Jacobson. For Disneyland, it had been created by fellow Imagineer Tony Baxter along with Bruce Gordon and John D. Stone.

There had to be some significant exterior color changes to blend into the WDW Frontierland color scheme (rather than the reddish Georgia-type coloring at Disneyland) and the music has more of a country-western feeling with banjos and harmonicas.

In the Disneyland version, there are significantly more Audio-Animatronic characters because they were rescued from the America

Sings attraction. In Florida, there are fewer such figures because they were expensive to build.

One character is unique to the Florida version. Before the big drop, a brown weasel exclaims in a high voice "Go FSU!" as he pops out of a hole in the ceiling. It is a reference to one of the Imagineer's alma mater, Florida State University.

The length of Magic Kingdom's flume is 2,600 feet with four drops, while the Disneyland flume is 2,640 feet with five drops.

However, at its core, the attraction is basically the same.

When new CEO Michael Eisner was given his first tour of Imagineering in 1984, Tony Baxter and the Splash Mountain model had been pushed into a back corner because there were so many other presentations championed by senior Imagineers, who had been invited to pitch them to Eisner.

While Eisner was being shown the projects high on the Imagineering agenda, his fourteen-year-old son, Breck, who had accompanied him on the visit, wandered over to the Splash Mountain model. Toward the end of his tour, Eisner noticed his son in the back and came over and found that his son really liked it.

Eisner decided that if his son was so intrigued with the model, others of that key demographic group would be as well, and gave it the green light.

Possible names proposed for the attraction included Song of the South Log Flume Ride, Zip-a-Dee-Doo-Dah, and Zip-a-Dee River Run.

At one point, Eisner looked at the model and said, "It's a mountain… you have a big splash at the end…it's Splash Mountain."

The Carousel of Progress

Walt Disney tried to convince General Electric to sponsor a new addition to Disneyland called Edison Square, just off of Main Street. In one of the buildings would be a show in four scenes that would have followed the story of a family over the decades as their lives were constantly improved by new inventions from General Electric.

That concept evolved into a theater where the seated audience revolved around the different stages. The attraction debuted at the 1964 New York World's Fair as the Carousel of Progress. It was so popular that, after the fair, it was relocated to Disneyland. Over 31 million guests experienced that version of the attraction from July 2, 1967, to September 9, 1973.

With the opening of the Magic Kingdom in Florida in October 1971, General Electric saw the opportunity to reach new customers with the show.

So, the still-popular Carousel of Progress closed and was relocated to Walt Disney World. At Disneyland, the carousel theater was used to house an entirely new show called America Sings, which opened in 1974.

The Carousel of Progress opened in Tomorrowland in Walt Disney World on January 15, 1975, along with another attraction, Space Mountain.

Extensive changes were made, from the elimination of the kaleidophonic screens in the prologue and epilogue, to the removal of the second-floor model of Progress City.

The theater no longer rotated clockwise, since there was no reason to position guests to go up a speed ramp to see the Epcot model on the upper floor. Now, the theater rotated counter-clockwise, with the exit being right next to the entrance.

There had been a change in leadership at General Electric, and the new powers-that-be felt that the iconic Sherman Brothers' song

"There's A Great Big Beautiful Tomorrow" was implying that G.E. customers should wait to purchase products because new and better things were coming just around the corner.

To satisfy GE, the Sherman Brothers composed a new song, "The Best Time of Your Life", often mistakenly referred to by its opening lyric "Now is the Time. Now is the Best Time." *Now* was the best time to buy products from General Electric instead of waiting for the beautiful tomorrow.

Not only was there a new theme song that was repeated throughout the show, but, once again, the final scene was updated to showcase the 1970s and a new voice cast recorded dialog for the entire performance. Other minor changes were made as well.

The final scene was again updated in 1981 to showcase the future of the 1980s. Early in 1985, General Electric decided not to renew its contract for the show, especially since it was sponsoring a similar show at the newly opened Epcot Center called Horizons that included some references to the carousel show.

So, when the Disney company next updated the show, it removed General Electric references (although the Hotpoint oven in Scene Two and the G.E. refrigerator in Scene Three remained).

Finally, in 1993, the entire attraction was rewritten and re-recorded with another new voice cast and re-named Walt Disney's Carousel of Progress, with the original theme song restored to the show.

Over the decades, this show changed more than any other Disney attraction. Some changes were relatively minor, such as Orville becoming a cousin rather than an uncle, while others have been more significant, including redecorating each scene to reflect the different seasons of the year.

The Birth of Space Mountain

Imagineer Marty Sklar remembered:

> My most difficult project? John Hench and I designed a ride to go inside a computer. We pitched it to all the lower folks and finally had to make the pitch to Sarnoff [David Sarnoff, the general manager of RCA].
>
> We put up the storyboards and we were told that Sarnoff always sat at the head of the table. So he could barely hear us and couldn't see the small storyboard drawings. He wrote a note and passed it to his vice president who passed it to a subordinate, etc., so it eventually got to me. The note read "Who are these people?"
>
> Nobody had told him why we were there or what we were doing. Defeated, I told Hench to come up with a project he wanted to do, and then we would try to sell RCA on it. So Hench came up with Space Mountain. When it came time to pitch, I insisted that Sarnoff sit in the middle of the table. The RCA people said "no" and I said, "We are talking to the person sitting in that chair."
>
> So they put a person guarding the chair and when Sarnoff came in they said, "The Disney people would like you to sit here." Sarnoff said, "Sure." Nobody had ever asked him before to sit anywhere else. They just assumed he wanted to sit at the head of the table. We sold the Space Mountain project.

Actually, the birth of Space Mountain began much earlier, in a series of meetings with Walt Disney in 1964. A design team headed by John Hench came up with a concept of redeveloping Tomorrowland in Disneyland with a space port that would feature a steel roller coaster with four separate tracks twisting and turning around each other in a serpentine fashion.

It was Walt who wanted the roller coaster to be in the dark so he could have precise control of the lighting and to project images on the interior walls.

Hench came up with the original drawing for the exterior of the attraction in 1965, and it is very similar to the final cone-shaped version familiar to park-goers today.

However, for a variety of reasons, Space Mountain did not debut with the new Tomorrowland in 1967. It wasn't until that meeting with RCA that the project was revived for the Magic Kingdom at Walt Disney World.

According to Disney publicity from 1975, the storyline of the attraction was that:

> Space Mountain captures the essence of Superspace. The expect-ant "space voyager" is transported through the space station launch portal, and through the vast man-made "solar field". He then orbits the glowing "satellite", becomes engulfed in spectacular nebulae, and plunges past myriads of strange stars and unknown galaxies to begin re-entry.

Former astronaut Gordon Cooper, commander of Mercury 9 and Gemini 5, provided personal consultation to help insure the authenticity of Space Mountain. He saw the attraction as "an attempt to give people the most realistic feeling of what they might encounter in space without actually taking a real space flight".

Space Mountain was the first indoor roller coaster where riders were in total darkness for the length of the ride so they couldn't tell where the drops or turns would occur. It was also the first thrill ride that was controlled by computers to maintain safety. Space Mountain was controlled by a pair of sensitive Nova 2/10 computers, which were able to respond instantaneously to any unexpected event by immediately halting all mechanical movement.

It was one of the handful of attractions that premiered at Walt Disney World before being replicated at other Disney theme parks.

The Country Bear Jamboree

Designed by Imagineer Marc Davis, the Country Bear Jamboree was originally intended to be an indoor attraction at the Bear Band Restaurant in Disney's planned Mineral King Ski Resort to be built in California in the 1960s.

As Imagineer Wathel Rogers recalled:

> After the Mineral King contract had been signed, Walt had an idea for entertainment after people had been skiing. Walt said, "What we are going to do is have a bear band and have them perform two or three programs of entertainment. We'll say that the bears had come out of the sequoias and we trained them to be entertainers."

When the Mineral King project fell through, the show premiered instead on opening day at the Magic Kingdom, where it received so much positive guest feedback that a replica was built at Disneyland in California with two theaters.

Marc Davis revealed:

> The drawings that Walt saw had all kinds of bears, not just a country band but a jazz band, a circus band. A lot of choices. I had a one-bear band in a red outfit with all these instruments he was playing.

When it was decided that the attraction was going to be Florida-specific, and since country-western music was so popular in that part of the country, the Floridian bears would make that kind of music.

The back story for the attraction was that Ursus H. Bear, after a restful hibernation, rounded up his musically inclined kinfolk and friends to put on a down-home celebration. WDW guests are invited to join in on the fun as the show continues to celebrate that first performance so many years ago.

Over the years, a variety of different shows with different costuming and songs have rotated through to help celebrate the seasons, including a Christmas Special show (introduced in 1984) and the Vacation Hoedown (introduced in 1986), but, nowadays, it is just the original show that still entertains the guests at Frontierland as it first did over four decades ago.

There are all sorts of wonderful details as well, including those bear-claw scratches on the floor of the waiting room, and bear pelts hanging up on the second floor outside that guests never seem to question.

According to WDW publicity, when the attraction opened Trixie was known as the Tampa Temptation. Big Al lived in a nearby swamp: "He didn't litter his cave with tin cans and paper cartons—he ate 'em."

Masters of ceremony Henry and Wendell are based on real life country-western singers Homer and Jethro, who wrote "Fractured Folk Song" and "Mama Don't Whoop Little Buford", both of which are performed in the show.

According to the publicity release:

> The Five Bear Rugs began playing music together when they were in first grade. Fifteen years later they were still playing—in fourth grade! Zeke plays the banjo and wears glasses—he's the only one who can read music. Fred plays the mouth harp and carries the tune (his wife says Fred is lazy, and a tune is the only thing he carries). Ted blows the white lightning jug, and Tennessee plays the one-stringed thing (he hopes one day to add more strings).

> Zeb plays fiddle, and Zeb's son Oscar accompanies his father on concert tours because Zeb's wife works (she models fur coats—always the same one—at a nearby boutique).

Once the attraction opened at Disneyland, North Woods bears, rather than Florida country bears, seemed appropriate for Bear Country, and later, Critter Country.

Spaceship Earth

When Epcot Center opened in 1982, the icon for the new Disney theme park was Spaceship Earth. It dominated the entrance, just as globe-like structures dominated the New York World's Fairs of 1939 and 1964–65.

The term "Spaceship Earth" was popularized by Buckminister Fuller, a designer, inventor, and early environmental activist. He envisioned that the planet, like a spaceship, continues to travel through the universe and people as the crew must work together to keep the spaceship in good shape.

Fuller also developed the intrinsic mathematics for a geodesic dome and received a patent for it in 1954.

Spaceship Earth is the largest geodesic sphere in the world, at 165 feet in diameter. It is 180 feet to the top and is covered by 954 triangular panels of alucobond (anodized aluminum on both sides heat-bonded with a polyethylene core in the center). It is supported fifteen feet off the ground by six steel legs driven deep into the ground. The structure seems to be floating.

Imagineer John Hench told reporter Laura Kavesh for her story in *The Orlando Sentinel* of October 24, 1982:

> The columns of Spaceship Earth are constructed to reach out like beckoning arms. I defy anyone who is depressed to still be depressed when they walk through there. We do all this from experience. Walt did it from intuition. It's designed to say, "You're okay. You're going to be okay." We as humans must make sense of things or we feel threatened.

Spaceship Earth is actually two separate spherical structures, one inside the other. The inner sphere is composed of 1,450 structural steel members arranged in a giant triangular fashion and is the weatherproof enclosure for the show. The inner core also contains decking at several levels and a spiral route for Spaceship Earth's ride system.

The outer sphere façade is held about two feet away from the inner core by aluminum hubs. A gutter was developed about mid-point on the sphere to collect rain water and channel it through the structure and its supporting legs to underground drains to eventually replenish the World Showcase lagoon. In that way, the water does not cascade down the side of Spaceship Earth onto the guests below.

To minimize air-conditioning costs, air cannons direct cool air only onto the 1,552 feet ride path so that guests don't feel the heat and humidity just a few feet away.

Before considering a geodesic sphere, different design structures were considered for Spaceship Earth including the Roman Parthenon, the dome of Saint Peter's Cathedral in the Vatican (150 feet high and 107 feet in diameter), and the 125-foot-diameter steel frame supporting a map of the world, like the one at the 1964–65 New York World's Fair. A golden geodesic dome was also seriously considered, inspired by the Expo '67 dome in Montreal.

Spaceship Earth was dedicated on October 1, 1982, the same day that Epcot Center first opened to the public. Chairman of Walt Disney Productions Card Walker said, "Communications is the beginning of understanding and thus fitting of the park's marquee attraction."

In less than a week, over 100,000 guests had ridden the attraction. Within the first year of operation, nearly 7.5 million guests had ridden Spaceship Earth, letting it claim the honor of the largest attendance of any attraction at Walt Disney World that year.

Inside Spaceship Earth

Spaceship Earth was not meant to be a museum, but many of the props and inscriptions are authentic reproductions of the originals. Imagineer John Hench insisted that the props in the attraction should be the closest approximation that could be created, even though few if any guests would be knowledgeable enough to know the difference.

Here are a handful of examples to look for on future visits to the Spaceship Earth:

Cro-Magnon Scene The animal skulls in this scene include a saber-toothed tiger, a lion, a cave bear, and two dire wolves. They were cast from molds of actual animals in the Paleolithic collection of the Page Museum in Los Angeles.

Egyptian Scene The hieroglyphics are accurate, and the gods Anubis, Soker, and Thoth are all represented. The translations of the hieroglyphics takes up several pages, but are all authentic to the time period.

Roman Scene The Latin inscription which appears at the entrance to the Roman scene comes from the first of the Twelve Tables of Roman Law that were codified about 451 B.C. and were regarded by later Romans as the foundation of all their laws. They were originally written on bronze tablets and placed in the marketplace for all to see and discuss.

The statue in the Roman scene is Emperor Augustus. The graffiti which appears on the walls in the Fall of Rome scene also appeared on the walls of ancient Pompeii and was taken from a collection of graffiti entitled *Loves and Lovers of Ancient Pompeii* by Professor Matteo Della Corte.

One example, "Quisquis amat pereat", translates to "May whoever loves perish!"

Islamic Scene The astronomer on the balcony holds a quadrant reproduced from photos of a 10th century Islamic quadrant supplied by the Metropolitan Museum of Art.

Medieval Scene Mary Robertson, a curator of rare manuscripts at the Huntington Library in San Marino, California, was consulted about the creation of manuscripts during the Middle Ages.

Gutenberg Scene Carey Bliss, a fellow curator of rare books at the Huntington Library, was consulted about the printing of the Gutenberg Bible. In this scene, the page Herr Gutenberg is examining was recreated from a page in the original Gutenberg Bible at the Huntington Library.

Renaissance Music Experts in the field of Renaissance musicology like Genette Foster from Occidental College in Los Angeles were engaged to consult and perform the music in this scene. The male musician is shown playing the lute and the female musician is playing the lira da braccio.

Steam Press/Newspaper The steam press, which dominates this scene, was designed from the actual patent drawings filed by William Bullock in 1863. The newspaper is a reproduction of the *New York Daily*.

Telegraph Scene The calendar is a copy of a calendar from 1867 by Hatch and Co. Lithographers supplied by the Smithsonian Institution, from the collection of Business Americana.

Telephone The magneto switchboard was fabricated from an actual model circa 1898, supplied by AT&T.

This is just a quick glimpse into the many layers of authentic detail that the Disney Imagineers painstakingly added to Spaceship Earth.

The Fountain

The Fountain of Nations? The Fountain of World Friendship? The CommuniCore (*Community* Core, not *Communication* Core) Fountain? Innoventions Fountain? Over the years, the fountain in the middle of Epcot has been called many different names both on fan websites and in official Disney press releases.

Whatever guests and cast members call the fountain, it is often used as a central meeting place landmark and photo location, with Spaceship Earth majestically looming in the background.

The iconic fountain has been a part of Epcot since opening day in October 1971. In fact, as a symbolic gesture of international cooperation and understanding, representatives from 22 countries each poured a gallon of water from their homelands into the fountain during the dedication ceremony of the park.

Today, every fifteen minutes, the fountain showcases water ballets where over two hundred shooters propel over fifty gallons of water up to one-hundred-and-fifty feet in the air.

There are seven different musical selections that rotate: the instrumental from the Air Battle sequence of Surprise in the Skies, a former daytime lagoon show at Epcot; "Day One" by John Tesh; the main title selection from the Disney live-action film, *Iron Will*; "Mickey's Finale" from a proposed Epcot show tentatively titled *Around the World with Mickey Mouse*; a selection from the Disney animated film *The Rescuers Down Under*; a selection from the Disney live-action film *The Rocketeer*; and "Standing in Motion" by Yanni.

It took three months of computer programming to design the seven different water ballets; in addition, at night over a thousand colored lights highlight the streams of water. It is the largest fountain on Disney property.

The fountain holds approximately 150,000 gallons of water with computer controlled pumps sending almost 30,000 gallons of that water, per minute, cascading down its tiered walls. It uses almost 35 miles of electrical wire. Chloride is too corrosive for this fountain, so Disney uses bromine to keep it clean and to ensure that no algae develops. The coins that are retrieved from the fountain, like others on property, are donated to local charities.

Running underneath the entire fountain is an underground work area that houses the pumps and computer systems, as well as a workshop for cast members who maintain the Epcot fountains. There is also a space with special lifts that are used beneath the stage area for performers and equipment.

The underground work area was built and then the fountain placed on top, with no planning for how to get new equipment down into the area. Over the years, the fountain has been damaged, such as when a temporary stage for performing elephants was put on top of it for the Epcot Center Daredevil Circus Spectacular in 1987.

In the 1980s, the fountain team at Walt Disney World included a young civil engineer whose thesis was on the behavior of turbulence-free water. That young engineer, Mark Fuller, later founded WET Design, now the premiere fountain company in the world.

Besides the Epcot fountain, Mark Fuller is also responsible for other Disney fountains including the leapfrog fountain at the Imagination pavilion. His greatest creation to date may be the water show at the Bellagio Hotel in Las Vegas.

Landscaping

Morgan "Bill" Evans was the original landscape architect for both Disneyland and Magic Kingdom (and the surrounding resort area). About landscaping Epcot, he stated:

> Epcot Center is going to be a tougher assignment than the Magic Kingdom. We're trying to create a typical landscape from foreign nations. We're trying to show trees typical of Japan, Canada, Mexico, and China. We have France, England, Italy, and Germany.
>
> Japan and China are particularly fascinating. There will be Chianthus Petusa, a Chinese fringe tree that is covered with white blossoms; the Japanese pagoda tree; the Chinese scholar tree; and the Japanese black pine, which looks like a giant Bonsai.

For the China Pavilion, Tony Virginia, the director of horticulture for Walt Disney World, acquired a hundred-year-old weeping mulberry he had found in New Jersey. The tree was fifteen-feet tall and very wide and distorted—the "look" sought for the area.

The tree was prepared for the long trip south using a procedure known as B & B, or ball and burlap. The root ball was held together with burlap. The tree was laid on its side aboard a flat-bed trailer. Trees as large as twenty-five-foot flowering pears from New Jersey had already been moved to Walt Disney World.

Some of the largest trees at Epcot (30–35 foot oaks) had to be transported vertically, aboard flat-bed trailers at Preview Boulevard at Lake Buena Vista (where they had been grown from saplings) and moved to a temporary holding area in the Epcot Center parking lot.

Routes were selected to avoid overhead wires, highway overpasses, and monorail beams (generally sixteen to eighteen feet above the ground on the route originally planned to move the trees). A permanent road avoiding the monorail was built.

While attempts were made to use trees authentic to the different countries, sometimes "look-alikes" had to be used to achieve the right appearance. Hemlock is a tree common to Canada and would be necessary to create an authentic landscape, but hemlocks would not survive in central Florida. "They need cold, cold winter weather, and they don't like humidity," stated Virginia.

Instead, Disney substituted Cedrus Deodora, a cedar native to the Himalayas that looked similar to the hemlock, but had the advantage of being able to thrive in central Florida.

Roughly 12,500 trees representing 125 species, over 100,000 shrubs of 250 species, 14 acres of Emerald Zoysia grass, and over three acres of annual flowers were planted for the opening of Epcot Center.

"And I won't tell you how much Argentina Bahia sod," said Virginia. That drought-resistant grass was used extensively "wherever we haven't installed irrigation".

Annuals, which normally last 45 days before replacement, began to be planted during mid-September 1982. Most of the annuals were planted in Future World, including 40,000 square feet of hillside beds at the Land pavilion. In total, 3.5 acres of annuals (over 40,000 plants) were planted before the park opened.

In the World Showcase Lagoon, on what was then known as "the islands of the world", slash pines predominated among a half-dozen island tree varieties so that it would "look like Florida woods—like we just carved it out", stated Bill Coan, the project landscape architect.

Morgan Evans recalled:

> It doesn't make any difference how carefully you contrive the planning or how good the material is or how efficiently it is all installed. The whole thing depends on maintenance and Walt Disney World is doing a first-class job. Walt Disney believed people would know the difference between good landscaping and bad landscaping and [Disney] is the best.

Japan Pavilion's Roy O. Disney Lantern

As Walt Disney's older brother Roy O. Disney stood on the marshy ground of Walt Disney World in the 1960s, all that could be seen were black water swamps often choked with decaying, tangled roots that would have to be removed, barren dunes of white sand, and an occasional grove of pine trees.

There were a handful of tethered gas balloons of different colors that also dotted the landscape to indicate the height and location of things to come, like Cinderella Castle.

One week after Walt Disney's death, Roy spoke to a group of Disney executives and creative staff in a projection room at the Disney Studio. At the age of 73, he was going to postpone his retirement. He told them:

> We are going to finish this park [in Florida], and we're going to do it just the way Walt wanted it. Don't you ever forget it. I want every one of you to do just exactly what you were going to do when Walt was alive.

A tribute to Roy stands just as quietly and unobtrusively as the man himself in the Japan Pavilion.

Emperor Hirohito of Japan was a huge fan of Mickey Mouse. He was given a Mickey Mouse watch as a gift during his special tour of Disneyland in 1975. For years, even on formal occasions, Hirohito was observed wearing the watch. In 1979, there was panic when the watch stopped ticking, and a concerned palace chamberlain rushed it to Tokyo experts specializing in American timepieces.

This situation was of such national concern to both Hirohito and the people of Japan that it was reported in *Time* magazine in its September 18, 1979 issue. Fortunately, the watch merely required a new battery.

When Walt Disney World opened in 1971, two Japanese companies were investigating the possibilities of having a Disneyland in Japan. Formal talks with lawyers began in 1974, with a contract finally being signed in 1979.

To help cement the friendship between Japan and Disney, Emperor Hirohito personally presented to Roy O. Disney, for the dedication of the Magic Kingdom, a stone Japanese lantern known as a Toro to light the way to success and happiness.

Toro is a stone lantern used to illuminate the grounds of Buddhist temples, Shinto shrines, Japanese gardens, and other locations that are steeped in tradition. The hollowed-out top piece is where a candle or oil lamp is placed. The most famous of these lanterns are the several thousand lining the entry to Nara Prefecture's Kasuga shrine.

For almost ten years, the gift was on display, without any placard, at the Polynesian Resort. However, with the opening of Epcot's World Showcase (as well as the construction of Tokyo Disneyland, which was only a year from completion), the stone lantern was moved to the Japan Pavilion, opposite the structure at the entrance that was inspired by the eighth-century pagoda found at Horyuji Temple in Nara.

The deer on the side of the lantern represents the famous Nara Deer Park adjacent to the Kasuga shrine.

Imagineers explain that there is no placard because "it is a story of the Disney parks but not of the story of Japan we are trying to represent".

Thousands of guests pass the lantern every day without realizing its story, but now you won't be one of them.

Germany Pavilion's Railway Garden

In 1995, for the Epcot International Flower and Garden Festival, the WDW horticulturists decided it would be fun to build a railway garden.

Railway gardens at the time were such a popular hobby that there was even a magazine, *Garden Railways*, dedicated to them. According to a Disney handout:

> As you can see, a lot of imagination has gone into the landscape here at the Germany railway garden. All of these things can be recreated in your own backyard with a little patience and creativity.

What the Disney horticulturists did not realize was that the 50-foot by 130-foot model garden layout would become so instantly popular with Disney guests that it would remain year round. In 2015, it celebrated its 20th anniversary.

In fact, subtle alterations are done to the layout during the different seasons, including adding Christmas decorations for the holidays. Multiple variations are often done throughout the year simply on the whim of the horticulturists and what plant material is available.

The three electric model trains that go through tunnels, over bridges, past a town and picture-postcard scenery are from a German company, Lehmann Gross Bahn (LGB, and German for "Lehmann's Big Train"). LGB introduced G-scale, 1.22.5, the standard for garden railways. The trains run on a 45mm gauge track.

A new magnetized track was installed in 2008 because pesky squirrels kept knocking the trains off of the tracks. Guest Relations, responding to guests' concerns, were always trying to locate someone to put the trains back on the tracks.

Since the space available was near the Germany Pavilion, Disney decided to do a recreation of the colorful Romantic Road (Romantische Strasse) in southern Germany from Fussen to Wurzburg.

Over six hundred years ago, this route was Germany's most prosperous trade route, and today, it takes travelers through a wonderland of turreted castles, towering cathedrals, and ancient walled towns, all seemingly unchanged since the Middle Ages.

Epcot's version includes a medieval castle set in a miniature Black Forest composed of cypress, juniper, and cedar. In addition, there is an alpine village, a large farm, a prosperous Bavarian town, vineyard, and a miniature orchard. There is also a 17th century monastery, with a gristmill and a sawmill across the river.

The railroad consists of three lines: a passenger line running between distant cities through the countryside to the Wurzburg stations and back, a freight train on a loop through the town and forest, and a rack locomotive climbing up the steep alpine grades and back down to Fussen.

If you are sharp-eyed, you might notice that on the front of one of the locomotives is the Blazon of Grisons (Graubunden), a Swiss canton, indicating that the train is actually Swiss and not German.

The primary concern for the Disney crew each morning is not with the little lizards that invade the setting like mini-Godzillas and sometimes hide inside the buildings. Every morning the first thing they have to do is check inside the tunnels because rabbits crawl into them during the night as a safe burrow and are reluctant to leave in the morning.

Special care has always been taken to maintain this simple, beautiful miniature gem that for two decades has brought great joy to Epcot guests.

Remembering Body Wars

The Star Tours and Body Wars attractions use a simulator (Rediffusion ATLAS-Advanced Technology Leisure Application Simulator) that consists of a cabin supported by six servo actuators ("legs").

The actuators are powered hydraulically and driven automatically using electrical drive signals received from a free-standing motion-control cabinet. The actuators provide "six degrees of freedom movement" so the cabin can be moved in planes representing heave, surge, and sway, and in axes representing pitch, roll, and yaw, independently or in any combination.

In fact, the success of Star Tours in 1987 inspired the Imagineers to try developing an "inner space" attraction of a miniaturized submarine-like probe journeying through a patient's body just like in the film *Fantastic Voyage* (1966) for the Wonders of Life pavilion at Epcot in 1989.

The new attraction was called Body Wars most likely because WDW guests called Star Tours the Star Wars ride, or just Star Wars.

The probe's captain, Jack Braddock (Tim Matheson from *Animal House*), set out on a fairly routine medical mission with a crew of civilian observers accompanying him. The submarine and crew were miniaturized by a "particle reducer" to the size of a single cell and beamed inside a human body to rendezvous with Dr. Cynthia Lair (Elisabeth Shue, who starred in Touchstone's *Adventures in Babysitting*), an immunologist who had also been miniaturized to study the body's response to a splinter lodged beneath the skin.

Unfortunately, the mission becomes a high-speed race against time when Dr. Lair is swept from the splinter site into the rush of the bloodstream.

Through the pounding chambers of the patient's heart and through the lungs' gale-force winds, the ship rode the body's current in an effort to rescue Dr. Lair. Even after she was safely on board, there are still problems when the ship loses power and heads toward the brain in search of emergency power and escape.

The film was directed by Leonard "Mr. Spock" Nimoy who had recently finished directing Touchstone's *Three Men and a Baby* (1987). With anatomical images produced by computer graphics and special effects film techniques, it was a remarkably realistic experience. Nimoy said:

> Even though *Body Wars* is the shortest film I've ever directed, it presented a new set of challenges. We had to take into account that the film will be shown inside a moving theater—the simulator. So, in order to intensify the sense of motion, we built a set that actually moves, and rocked it during filming to match the pitching and rolling of the simulator.

When the ride was being programmed, an Imagineer watched the film repeatedly while moving a computer joystick to indicate movement and to synchronize the ride and the film.

Since the story of the attraction was that guests were in the bloodstream, the Imagineers programmed in movement to mimic the beat of a pulse. That additional movement may be the one that unsettled countless guests who had survived a similar experience on Star Tours without any ill effects.

Some Disney Imagineers felt that it was just the images of being inside a human body with all the yucky "blood and guts" that generated feelings of unease.

The attraction closed when the Wonders of Life Pavilion closed on January 1, 2007. The simulators were eventually stripped for parts for the Star Tours attraction at Disney's Hollywood Studios, so it would be difficult for Body Wars to once again be brought back to life and rush through the circulatory and respiratory systems and make guests queasy.

The Original Figment and Dreamfinder

While Dreamfinder and Figment were there at the opening of Epcot October 1982, their famous ride, Journey Into Imagination, did not officially open at the Imagination Pavilion until March 5, 1983.

For more than 15 years, Dreamfinder delighted guests of all ages in the attraction itself as an Audio-Animatronic figure and also as a walk-around character carrying a mischievous Figment puppet who might snatch a hat from a guest and fling it in the air.

Dreamfinder and Figment were considered the official spokes-characters for Epcot. Yet, after 1998, Dreamfinder disappeared, and Figment almost vanished as well.

Who were Figment and Dreamfinder? The little purple dragon, Figment, was the physical representation of "a figment of the imagination". Dreamfinder was his husky human companion and friend with a full red beard, long blue coat, black top hat, and broad smile, supposedly modeled after the physical appearance of Imagineer Joe Rohde.

Figment and Dreamfinder were born in a concept for a planned-but-never-built section of Disneyland to be called Discovery Bay. In that area there was to be Professor Marvel's Gallery of Illusion, "a fascinating visit with the foremost collector of the exotic, weird, and whimsical from all over the world", according to a press release from October 1976.

Entering through a sideshow wagon, guests would find themselves in a Carousel of Progress-type revolving theater where an Audio-Animatronic Professor Marvel would display all manner of oddities that he has assembled, including his collection of dragons.

A small statue of the magnificent white-bearded and mustached Marvel was built with a black top hat, gold vest, red tie, and monocle.

Cradled in his right arm was a small green dragon that Marvel bred as a hobby.

At that time, every available resource of the Disney company had been redirected to the Epcot and Tokyo Disneyland projects, and the Discovery Bay project was shelved. Imagineer Steve Kirk remembered:

> I was in my office. [Imagineer] Tony Baxter was in with the Kodak folks as being potential sponsors for some kind of Epcot pavilion. He ran into my office in the middle of this meeting and said, "Can I borrow the Dreamkeeper [the original name for Dreamfinder]?"
>
> And he grabbed the statue and took it in to them to show it to them. They said, "That's great, do we get the dragon, too?" The only issue was that, at the time, the dragon was painted green. Figment was green. And Kodak thought that represented a little too much of a Fuji Film (Kodak's chief competitor, who used the color green prominently on its packaging) connection, so he turned purple as a result of that.

Tony Baxter recalled:

> [Dreamfinder] was a Santa Claus type who is wise and older and knows all the great things, a great thinker. But we needed a child-like character that had like a one-second attention span and was a little crazy.

To provide the voice for Dreamfinder, WED hired actor Chuck McCann who based the voice of Dreamfinder on actor Frank Morgan as the mighty wizard in MGM's *The Wizard of Oz* (1939). Actor Billy Barty did the voice for Figment.

Actor Ron Schneider appeared as Dreamfinder with a Figment puppet on opening day when he was interviewed by Bryan Gumbel on NBC's *Today* show. Later, Steve Taylor became Schneider's understudy, and then took over the role full-time for almost fifteen years when Schneider went on to other projects.

Taylor was significantly shorter than Schneider, so it was just assumed that, like Figment, the Dreamfinder could be any size he wanted. That's the true power of imagination.

The Purple Martins

During the annual Epcot Flower and Garden Festival, purple martins, the largest of the North American swallows, return to comfy white homes behind the Mouse Gear shop to start new families.

Some guests imagine that those white PVC gourds with an alphabet letter on them are cameras or special lighting fixtures on a white pole, but they are actually safe havens for birds who sometimes have to battle other sparrows and starlings for the treasured space.

The letters help identify each gourd for documentation by the Animal Programs team at Walt Disney World.

Purple martins are dependent on man-made housing to nest, a situation that has existed for hundreds of years when local Native Americans first hollowed out actual gourds (instead of the artificial ones used most often today) and hung them on trees.

As part of the Disney company's commitment to conservation efforts, there are approximately 60 houses at Epcot and between 160–180 houses backstage at Disney's Animal Kingdom.

The program first began more than seventeen years ago as part of a backyard bird garden exhibit for the Epcot Flower and Garden Festival, but was kept to delight guests and to provide a habitat for these birds, whose future at that time was threatened.

James Mejeur, a zoological manager at Disney's Animal Kingdom, has been in charge of maintaining the Walt Disney World colonies of purple martins since 2005. He said:

> It is a popular myth that we encourage the purple martins to return to Epcot because they control the mosquito population. Actually, the purple martins fly higher than mosquitoes. If the purple martins were dependent on eating mosquitoes, they would have to eat tens of thousands a day and even then they would probably still be hungry.
>
> The birds are completely dependent on humans for homes and have been for centuries. They communicate with each other so they know

where the man-made homes will be. The other birds follow them in. We have to check the houses two to three times a week. We watch when the eggs are laid and when they hatch and contact a national data bank. They are vulnerable to other more aggressive birds like starlings who will fight them for the nesting opportunities.

Sometimes squirrels will want to kick them out and take over the housing or endanger the eggs. In addition, we have to check for feather mites because they may weaken the chicks or irritate them to the point that they will leave the nest and fall to their death. We sometimes have to change out the entire nest with new material.

The older birds arrive first, sometimes as early as around Christmas, because they are smart enough to realize that the early bird gets the prime homes for nesting. They come in waves. The younger birds who arrive later get what's left. With age comes experience that helps with survival. Generally, by the second week in January, they have all arrived.

There is a purple martin community out there and we all keep in touch online and are in a friendly competition to see the first one. By late July, the purple martins are gone again. During the period they are here, we help fledge hundreds of chicks, increasing the endangered population. Guests love purple martins because they are associated with happy memories and are a way to connect with nature.

For me personally, they are the soundtrack to the wonderful summers I spent with my grandparents on their farm.

The Chinese Theater

When it officially opened on May 1, 1989, former CEO Michael Eisner described what was then-called Disney-MGM Studios as "The Hollywood That Never Was But Always Will Be".

The park was to be a representation of the Hollywood seen in the movies and on postcards and in fan magazines; not a geographical location, but a state of mind. At the time, the actual Hollywood was a fairly dangerous location and had fallen into a state of seediness.

However, in order to achieve the illusion of the Golden Age of Hollywood, there had to be some iconic landmarks that guests immediately associated with that fabled location, including the legendary Grauman's Chinese Theater.

Grauman's Chinese Theater was a classic movie palace located at 6925 Hollywood Boulevard that was famous for its forecourt where movie stars left impressions of their handprints and footprints in cement, as well as its many star-studded movie premieres.

Walt Disney was a friend of Sid Grauman, even caricaturing him in the Mickey Mouse cartoon *Mickey's Gala Premiere* (1933). Grauman was the theater's managing director until his death. The theater premiered the first Technicolor Silly Symphony, *Flowers and Trees*, in 1933. Both *Mary Poppins* (1964) and *The Jungle Book* (1967) had their premieres there, and artifacts from both of those events are in the two glass display enclosures in front of the theater.

The Disney Imagineers used the original blueprints of the 1927 Meyer and Holler building for reference, and the façade was built to its full scale of ninety-six-feet tall, rather than the forced perspective of the other buildings in the park. The structure was meant to serve a similar function as the iconic castles at other Disney theme parks.

One of the few adjustments was that the ticket booth in front of the original theater was moved to the side for the Disney version so as not to block the entrance to the Great Movie Ride.

The 22-ton central roof section is 45 feet tall and was constructed separately and hoisted into place by a crane as a finishing touch.

The plaque on the outside of the building says that the original theater opened in 1928. It actually opened in 1927, and some claim it is not a foolish mistake, but an intentional gag by the Imagineers because there is 1,928 feet of track in the attraction.

One of the challenges facing Disney was that it had not produced classic live-action films in the 1930s and 1940s that it could use to re-create the era. In 1985, Disney signed a contract with MGM/UA (Metro Goldwyn Mayer/United Artists) to use up to 250 films from its movie library.

Some series were considered so valuable on their own that they had to be negotiated separately, including *The Wizard of Oz*, *Singing in the Rain*, *Gone with the Wind*, and the James Bond films.

That's why the final film montage has just seconds featuring Sean Connery as Bond. A room devoted to the tornado that carried little Dorothy to the land of Oz had to be redesigned to feature the storm from Disney's *Fantasia* (1940). It was too expensive to use the storm from *Wizard of Oz* because the licensing fee Disney had to pay MGM/UA was tied to the length of time the material was shown.

Several celebrities, including Maureen O'Sullivan, Harrison Ford, and Dick Van Dyke, whose films are represented in the attraction, placed their handprints and signatures in the forecourt cement when the Great Movie Ride originally opened.

The Great Movie Ride

In initial discussions, one of the ideas suggested for the Great Movie Ride was to have live celebrity impersonators inside interacting with the guests, but it was decided that Audio-Animatronic figures would not only be more cost-effective, but would provide a more consistent show experience.

Imagineers wined and dined Gene Kelly before showing him his doppelganger for the ride, and the result was that Kelly signed off immediately. (When the ride debuted, Kelly's umbrella was open, but the water occasionally splattered off of it and hit the guests.)

Actor James Cagney's family was unhappy with his attire in the gangster scene from his classic film *Public Enemy* (1931), so they gave the Imagineers one of Cagney's actual tuxedos to make him appear more "classy".

The prop newspapers scattered around Patrick J. Ryan's bar that cannot be seen clearly by the guests are actually copies of the local Florida paper, *The Orlando Sentinel*. The puddles on the ground are not real liquid and often accumulate dust and need to be wiped during maintenance, as do the "horse puddles" in the Western scene.

Liza Minnelli, the daughter of actress Judy Garland, supplies the voice for the character of Dorothy in the Wizard of Oz scene. Ingrid Bergman does not speak in the Casablanca scene because her family would not give permission to use her voice, even though Bergman's grandchildren have been brought through the attraction several times to see their grandmother.

By the way, Humphrey Bogart was shorter than Bergman in real life, but his figure is taller in the attraction.

John Wayne's voice was impersonated by actor Doug McClure. When he was alive, Wayne had heard McClure impersonating him and apparently approved of it. When the ride originally opened, the figure did wear the real belt buckle that the actor wore in the movie

Red River (1948). However, as soon as that information became public knowledge, it was stolen and a replica took its place.

The little band that the Wayne figure wears on his right hand was one that Wayne was given for good luck when he visited Vietnam, so the figure does indeed wear something authentic from the actor.

The cards on the floor by the Clint Eastwood figure originally had numbers on them, but during a rehab were changed out to cards with just the suits, which were more authentic to the time period. Eastwood's figure does not represent a specific scene from any of his films. The figure was a next-to-last-minute replacement for actor Lee Marvin, when his family refused to authorize his Oscar winning portrayal of a gunfighter sitting on a tipsy horse from the comedy *Cat Ballou* (1965).

Maureen O'Sullivan, who played Jane in the movie *Tarzan the Ape Man* (1932), came to Orlando and got a picture taken with her Audio-Animatronics double on the elephant.

When her figure was built in California and ready to be shipped to Florida, it was wrapped in clear plastic and completely unclothed (since the clothes would be added when the figure was installed so that they would hang properly), and many people made unnecessary trips to the loading dock just to check it out.

In June 2015, the attraction saw many changes with the new sponsorship of Turner Classic Movies, including movie historian Robert Osborne not only hosting a longer pre-show film, but also narrating the ride. In addition, there is a different movie montage as the finale.

The Cameraman Statue

Oddly, the dedication plaque for Disney's Hollywood Studios is not near the front of the park, but at the end of Hollywood Boulevard, just over to the left in a fenced-in grassy circle.

Directly to the right of the plaque is the *Cameraman* statue. This statue was originally sculpted by father and son Aldo and Andrea Favilli in 1991.

Andrea Favilli received his formal education at the Art Center College of Design, where he graduated with honors in 1986. He has stated that he felt his art education truly began when he was a child growing up in Rome as he began drawing, painting, and sculpting under the tutelage of his father, Aldo, who was working as a motion picture art director at Cinecittà Studios.

Upon his graduation from school, Andrea worked as a product designer for a variety of clients, including Mattel, Dakin, and Applause. In particular, it was his creative involvement with the characters of the Dancing Raisins and Domino Pizza's "Noid" that caught the attention of the Disney company.

He joined Walt Disney Imagineering in 1987 as a lead concept designer working on a range of projects worldwide, including ones for Disneyland, the Magic Kingdom, Epcot Center, Typhoon Lagoon, Disney/MGM Studios, Pleasure Island, Disney's Animal Kingdom, Tokyo Disneyland, and Disneyland Paris.

In 1992, Andrea opened Favilli Studio, and, of course, the Disney company was one of his clients, as was Roy E. Disney and Shamrock Holdings.

In fact, the DHS *Cameraman* statue is based on the original statue that Andrea made with his father that is located at 4411 West Olive Avenue across from Gate 2 of the Warner Brothers Studio in Burbank.

It was commissioned by Roy E. Disney and Shamrock Holdings, and was placed there in 1991 to celebrate the art of film-making in the heart of the film-making capital of the world. The plaque reads: "He envisioned dreams that others might share."

The man in the statue is a generic 1920s/1930s film-maker, not based on anyone in particular, especially not a young Walt Disney, as some have claimed. It reflects the transition period when silents disappeared and talkies took over.

Andrea was also responsible for sculpting the Disney Legends award, the American Teacher award, and the Frank G. Wells award for the Disney company, as well as the Transpacific Yacht Race New Course Record trophy for Roy E. Disney.

A replica of the Burbank statue was later placed in Disney's Hollywood Studios in 1995 with a plaque that states: "Movies are a medium of expression like a symphony orchestra, or a painter's brush on canvas. —Walt Disney."

The placement of the statue at DHS was not just to honor film-making, but to suggest that the guests are being filmed as they enter the park and are part of the motion picture they are about to experience.

At the feet of the cameraman are a director's megaphone and an open script that includes the names of people who inspired Andrea, including Herbert Dickens Ryman and Lucille Ryman Carroll (Andrea is a retired board member of the Ryman-Carroll Foundation), Roy E. Disney and Patricia Disney, Marty Sklar, and Andrea's father, Aldo.

Gertie the Dinosaur

Dinosaur Gertie's Ice Cream of Extinction was built as a tribute to Gertie the Dinosaur, one of the very first animated cartoon stars, and a cartoon that inspired both a young Walt Disney and Ub Iwerks to pursue animation.

Gertie first amazed vaudeville audiences in 1914 when she was projected life-size onto a movie screen and shared the stage with her creator, Winsor McCay, a popular newspaper cartoonist who was responsible for the legendary *Little Nemo in Slumberland* Sunday comic strip.

McCay had to do more than 10,000 drawings to make approximately five minutes of animation. There were no schools or books that taught animation, so he had to invent a method to do it.

McCay used this innovative animated short film as part of his vaudeville act. McCay would come on stage dressed in a tuxedo with a huge bullwhip like an animal trainer and tell Gertie to lift her leg, and on a big movie screen to the side of him, Gertie would lift her leg.

He would pull out a big apple and pretend to toss it to her, and on screen she grabbed an animated apple and ate it as McCay palmed the actual prop.

At the end of the act, McCay would walk up to the screen and an animated version of himself would get on Gertie's head and they would leave the scene together. The real McCay had already walked behind the screen while people watched Gertie.

As the plaque near Dinosaur Gertie's in Disney's Hollywood Studios states:

> The themed style of the building is known as "California Crazy" architecture. It became popular in the 1930s and was designed to attract the attention of potential customers in a big way.

Back in the 1930s and 1940s, the time frame for the park, people believed it was the Ice Age that killed off the dinosaurs. That's why it is the ice cream of "extinction" rather than "distinction" that is being sold at this location.

Gertie is so cold that steam occasionally comes out of her nostrils. The top part of her back is covered with snow.

In her original concept sketch, and when she first appeared in the park, the green words "Ice Cream" covered with snow curved over the top of her back, but over the years, that lettering was removed.

Gertie is in a lake because, in her animated cartoon, she is by a large lake throughout. At one point, she tosses a mammoth into the lake. In another sequence, she almost falls in after she drinks the entire lake dry.

In her film, she is white, but she is colored green at the park because the first movie posters of her were colored green, since at the time people thought that dinosaurs were green or brown like lizards.

Gertie is located at Disney's Hollywood Studios because she is considered the first example of what is known as "personality" or "character" animation—even though she is just a creation of pen and ink, she seems to have a distinct personality with a wide range of emotions, from being shy to being stubborn, and as a result seems almost real.

In fact, follow the pathway to a set of steps behind her, and you will see on the walkway where Gertie's feet have cracked the cement as she walked into the lake and left an imprint. When the park first opened, those same footprints were evident in the landscaping, so it looked as if Gertie walked slowly to her comfortable location.

On the Trail of the Rocketeer

As part of the summer 1991 promotion for Touchstone Pictures' *The Rocketeer* (1991), a live Rocketeer lifted off by jet pack and flew briefly above the Chinese Theater courtyard during each evening's presentation of the Sorcery in the Sky fireworks show.

Even today, on the left side of the forecourt with the cement hand-prints and autographs of other actual celebrities, visitors can find the imprints of the boots and "blast marks" of the Rocketeer in cement, reminiscent of a scene planned, but never shot for the original film.

On the left-side aisle that leads to the main dining room in the Sci-Fi Dine-In Theater, down to the right and near the bottom, is the black-and-gold front cover of the South Seas Club menu—secured under plexiglass. The South Seas Club was the scene of a showdown between the Rocketeer and villain Neville Sinclair and his thugs.

Wandering a little farther down, just before the entrance to the main dining area, high on the left wall is a rocket pack that was used in the actual film. Directly to the right and about waist level, and also protected by plexiglass, is a prop copy of the *Los Angeles Examiner* newspaper with the headline, "Who is the Rocketeer?"

When Disney-MGM Studios opened in 1989, the Echo Lake area had the Lakeside News, which sold comic books and publications like old issues of *Life* magazine and other souvenirs. By 1991, to theme in with *The Rocketeer*, it became Peevy's Polar Pipeline, featuring "Frozen Coca-Cola Concoctions" as well as soft drinks, water, and snacks.

The interior of the location is filled with welding tanks, gauges, and other mechanical items that might have been found in Ambrose "Peevy" Peabody's workshop in 1938. Peevy was the best friend of Cliff Secord, the Rocketeer. Very prominently displayed on the left-side wall is a Rocketeer helmet, and below it is a rocket jet pack.

Many versions of the Rocketeer helmet were made for the film because, in those days before CGI became common, the stunts were always performed by live stunt men or through the use of miniature models. The helmet showcased at Peevy's is obviously a stunt helmet because it is wider and has larger eye lenses.

This helmet was meant to form around a sky-diving helmet and designed to be easy to "break away" in case an emergency arose during the stunt. For that reason, the helmet is wider than the "hero helmet" (the prop used by the main actor and in close-ups), and there is a slight splitting along the side seams common among the stunt helmets for the film. The eye lens area is larger to give the stunt person greater visibility. Directly below the helmet is a rocket jet pack also used during filming.

Moving closer to the posted menus on either side of Peevy's will reveal the blueprints for the rocket jet pack behind the items listed for sale. That's why the menu boards are blue.

In the early 1990s, larger prop items like Cliff Secord's GeeBee flying racer and the Bulldog Diner were prominent items on the Backlot Tour. In the queue for that attraction were other rocket packs and helmets next to the Lucky Lindy statue from the film.

While *The Rocketeer* was not as financially successful as Disney hoped, it has gained a huge cult following during the past two decades.

Star Tours: The Adventures Continue

Star Tours: The Adventures Continue debuted at Walt Disney World in 2011 and featured a different storyline than its previous incarnation. According to Disney publicity:

> It has been a long time since the end of the Clone Wars, and the evil Sith Lord Darth Vader continues to tighten his grip on the empire as the galaxy moves closer to the brink of a great civil war.

> A new intergalactic spaceline, Star Tours, seeks to preserve unrestricted intergalactic travel in this age of tyranny. Freedom fighter Captain Raymus Antilles has assigned two droids, C-3PO and R2-D2, to help launch the spaceline, fueling Imperial suspicion that Star Tours is part of the Rebel Alliance.

> Star Tours is about to open its first intergalactic space terminal in the Earth System as rumors of a fearsome weapon of mass destruction dash all hope for peace and freedom in the galaxy...

Depending upon which of the combinations that are randomly selected during the flight, guests will visit either the ice planet Hoth, Tatooine for a podrace, Kashyyyk (the home planet of the Wookies, which was a suggestion of John Lasseter), Naboo, Coruscant, or the Death Star above the planet Geonosis.

Sharp-eyed Disney or *Star Wars* fans may catch a quick glimpse of some possible destinations that were abandoned, or may give an indication of possible future adventures.

During the launch sequence, guests can see other Starspeeders painted with different color schemes and logos than the one they are on, and an Aurebesh letter emblazoned on the side of each.

Just like the airports we are familiar with today, this busy spaceport has other spacelines using the facilities en route to other destinations. Despite the rise of the galactic empire, interstellar travel is still a thriving industry. Different tour companies, like Star Tours, carry tourists to the distant corners of the galaxy for exotic vacations.

Those other Starspeeder 1000s are:

Dantooine Express White with a brown diagonal at the rear with the letter "dora". Dantooine Express provides tours of the grasslands, rivers, and lakes on Dantooine, located in the Raioballo sector of the Outer Rim and far removed from most galactic traffic. On the tour, visitors see native wildlife, including the kath hound, the iriaz, the kinrath, and the graul.

Tatooine Transit Solid blue with a white letter "nern". Tatooine Transit provides tours of the planet Tatooine in the Outer Rim Territories. This dangerous area is controlled by the Hutts, but travelers can still visit popular sites such as Mos Espa, the Dune Sea, moisture farms, and even the infamous Mos Eisley Cantina.

Bespin Direct White with a brownish top with white letters outlined in red: "wesk", "dora", "isk". Bespin Direct offers tours of the gas planet in the Bespin system, located in the Outer Rim Territories. Tours include the refinery production facilities of the tibanna gas mines and the famous floating Cloud City luxury resort.

Naboo Spacelines Gold with a brown circle at the back with a white "nern". Naboo Spacelines travels to Naboo near the Outer Rim territories. It is a largely unspoiled world with large plains, swamps, and seas. Tours include a visit to the capital city of Theed or the underwater Gungan city of Otoh Gunga.

Air Alderaan White with a brown "aurek" letter at the back. Air Alderaan offers tours of the second planet in the Alderaan system. This planet is considered the "Shining Star" of the Core Worlds. Wild grasslands, old mountain ranges, and large oceans dominate the planet's land surface. One of the highlights of the tour is a visit to the capital city of Aldera.

Mama Melrose

Hidden away in the back of Disney's Hollywood Studios, and often overlooked by guests, is an Italian eatery called Mama Melrose's Ristorante Italiano. There is an interesting story behind how it got its location and its name.

When the park opened in 1989, it was going to showcase Jim Henson's Muppets in the back of the park where Mama Melrose's is located today.

The never-built Great Gonzo's Pizza Pandemonium Parlor would have been run by Gonzo and Rizzo the Rat. Things would constantly be going horribly wrong both offstage in the kitchen and in the dining area itself to entertain guests as they dined on Italian food and watched the antics on monitors by their tables.

When Henson passed away in early 1990, negotiations with the Disney company fell apart and the Imagineers conceived of a different kind of Italian restaurant.

According to the official storyline, a young girl in a small Sicilian village in Italy fell in love with the magic of Hollywood movies while she worked in her father's restaurant. Her father loved her dearly and shared with her all his special secret recipes that made his restaurant such a favorite place for people to eat.

At the age of sixteen, she sailed for America and found a movie career as "a stand-in for actresses with names like Gina, Sophia, and Anna".

While she waited with the other extras between scenes, she cooked up Italian dishes with a little California flavor for her friends. Realizing that her dreams of stardom were not coming true, she opened her own Italian restaurant on the back lot.

The new restaurant provided meals for a variety of Hollywood types, from actors to the film crew to producers and directors. Her flamboyant approach to life reminded the Hollywood studio moguls of the town's eccentric Melrose Avenue, so they nicknamed her "Mama Melrose".

It was a name that was so descriptive of her that it stuck, and even today no one can recall what her actual name might have been.

The restaurant became the location "where Italy meets California in the heart of the Backlot". It was housed in a warehouse that was used for storing film equipment, with an exterior façade prized by motion pictures studios for shooting films based in New York City's Little Italy.

Mama and her friends converted the interior with what little funds they had into a family restaurant, but that is why the interior still has industrial-looking light fixtures, high ceilings with clearly visible air ducts, brick walls covered with graffiti, and worn floor boards in places from the moving of heavy film equipment.

To make the massive space appear more inviting, Mama decorated with whatever she had available: Hollywood memorabilia that she gathered during her years in the film business and numerous items from Italy in order to remember and honor her family back home.

That is the reason that the interior is such a mishmash of everything from Italian paintings to Hollywood movie posters to records of famous Italian singers to pennants of California sports teams to license plates and cooking utensils.

It suggests the home of a mother who accumulated many knick knacks as physical reminders of her many memories.

And, according to the Imagineers, that is how this charming restaurant got its name and unique interior design.

Sid Cahuenga

Sid Cahuenga's One-of-a-Kind Antiques and Curios shop, the home of Tinseltown Treasures at the front of Disney's Hollywood Studios, has been a familiar site to park guests since opening day in May 1989.

While today the location is a MagicBand Service Center, it originally sold items that included posters of Disney movies, black-and-white portrait photos of Walt Disney, pressbooks from Disney films, celebrity autographed photos, books, and costuming.

In fact, for sixteen years up to 2005, guests had the opportunity to meet and have their pictures taken with the friendly Sid Cahuenga himself. Actually, Sid was talented performer Danny Dillon whose signed and framed photo once hung prominently just inside the establishment's front door.

Dillon, who passed away at the age of eighty-two, was so iconic as Sid that he was never replaced in that role after his death.

The name "Sid" was inspired by iconic showman Sid Grauman, who owned and operated Grauman's Chinese Theater on Hollywood Boulevard as well as other popular movie theaters like the Egyptian. The name "Cahuenga" came from Cahuenga Boulevard, a major cross street that leads directly into the heart of Hollywood.

According to the back story created by Disney Imagineering, Sid Cahuenga was a big movie fan. With his wife, he relocated from the Midwest to the Hollywood of the 1920s where they bought some land and built their small home.

Unlike other buildings at Disney's Hollywood Studios, Sid's is not based on any particular structure, but instead is faithful to an architectural style associated with that time period.

The story behind the real Janes House built in 1903 on Hollywood Boulevard influenced the story of Sid Cahuenga's shop about a Hollywood residence that was turned into a business after other commercial structures were built around it.

Once Hollywood grew in the area where the house was built, real estate developers tried desperately to buy the now-valuable property from Sid, but he always refused. He and his wife did not want to move, and they liked being in the heart of all the expanded activity.

With a steady stream of tourists and shoppers now filling the street, Sid decided to make some extra money by displaying his collection of movie memorabilia that he had accumulated over the years.

He placed these items for sale on his front porch and front yard, just like an expensive garage sale. He was so successful that he expanded his business by transforming a few rooms in the front of his house into a store. He propped up items on bureaus, tables, and even the fireplace.

He realized he needed to replenish the one-of-a-kind items he was selling, so he got a large black flatbed truck, which he often parked next to his home. He would use the truck to buy surplus items from the movie studios or he'd rummage through dumpsters behind the studios to recover items that had been thrown away.

Look in the back of the truck and see some interesting items, including a figure from the Magic Kingdom's defunct 20,000 Leagues Under the Sea attraction.

Sid made many friends in the twenty years he lived in Hollywood, and some of those stars were only to happy to sign photos or give things to Sid, which he promptly put up for sale.

Sid and his wife made a good living for decades until their deaths.

Echo Park

On the first 1989 guide maps, the area at Disney-MGM Studios was referred to as Lakeside Circle. However, it was meant to be an homage to the real Echo Park that was built and opened in Los Angeles in 1895.

In fact, there is an archway and stairway for the Echo Lake Apartments near the Prime Time Café, and all the names on the mailboxes are references to Imagineers involved in the design of the park.

Before the development of Hollywood as the motion picture capital of the world, most of the Los Angeles film industry was centered in the Echo Park area, including Mack Sennett's Keystone Studios located on Keystone Street (now part of Glendale Boulevard).

Sennett was known for his silent movie comedies, in particular those starring the frantic, inept Keystone Kops, as well as Charlie Chaplin, and often used the park as the perfect setting for some of those wacky comedies. The Keystone Clothiers building stands at the entranceway to the area as a clever reference to Mack Sennett.

Just a few feet from the street sign that says "Keystone Street" is Peevy's Polar Pipeline. The architectural inspiration for the façade of this building was a fire station on Pasadena Avenue in Lincoln Heights built in 1940, but still in operation today.

To the right side of Peevy's is a door with the logo for the Holly-Vermont Realty Office. This was Walt Disney's first studio in Hollywood. Former Disney archivist Dave Smith wrote:

> Walt moved down the street on October 8, 1923, to 4651 Kingswell, and there in the back of a real estate office set up the first Disney studio. A contract was signed for the Alice Comedies on October 16, 1923, the official date of the beginning of the Disney Studio.

Walt told the owners of the office that he only needed enough room "to swing a cat in" and could only afford a maximum of ten dollars a month. He was given a room at the back of the real estate office.

In February 1924, the Disney brothers moved their studio into the empty storefront next to the real estate office. The address was 4649 Kingswell Avenue, and on the plate glass window was emblazoned in gold leaf the name "Disney Bros. Studio".

The sign in the upper window listing space for rent suggests that Walt and Roy have already moved out.

The Art Deco Hollywood and Vine, the so-called "cafeteria to the stars", is modeled after a cafeteria that once stood at 1725 North Vine, near Hollywood Boulevard. Before the dawn of fast food, these cafeterias (like Clifton's Cafeteria) provided actors, as well as Walt and Roy themselves, with inexpensive and varied choices.

Over the eatery is a window indicating the office of "Eddie Valiant. Private Investigations. All Crime. Surveillance. Missing Person." There is also a symbol of a magnifying glass with an eye in it, a reference to "private eye". Next to that window is an outline of Roger Rabbit bursting through the blinds and the window, just like in the famous scene in the movie *Who Framed Roger Rabbit* (1988) that was set in 1947 Hollywood.

In addition, atop the Holly-Vermont building is a huge billboard advertising the fictional Maroon Studios with an image of Roger and Jessica Rabbit with Baby Herman in a design reminiscent of the title card at the beginning of their cartoon shorts.

The Tree of Life

The Tree of Life was designed to capture the essence of the park with its diversity of animals and the majesty of nature.

The animals are not supposed to look as if they were carved into the surface of the tree. They are supposed to seem as if they grow out of it organically. It was designed to be reminiscent of looking up into the clouds and seeing the shapes of animals.

No one had ever built a tree this large. It is 145 feet tall, and the branches span 165 feet across with more than 103,000 translucent, five-shades-of-green leaves that were individually placed and actually sway in the wind because each branch unit is encircled by a giant expansion joint.

Disney commissioned a wind tunnel study for the branches that determined they could withstand a blow of nearly 100 miles per hour. The leaves are four different shapes and sizes, each more than a foot long, made out of a special plastic called Kynar. The bottom trunk is fifty feet wide. The Tree of Life is made up of 45 secondary branches leading to 756 tertiary branches leading to 7,891 end branches.

The branches had to appear random, but the cost of sculpting each one individually would have been cost-prohibitive. Using a computer, the Imagineers were able to come up with two types of secondary branches that could be hooked to two types of tertiary branches that could be randomly assembled, turned, and adjusted to create natural shapes.

The branches were assembled on the ground and then carried over and plugged into their appropriate spots by a huge crane.

The final look of the Tree of Life was based on a particular bonsai tree that the design team found at Epcot's International Flower and Garden Festival.

Eventually, it was decided to use an oil rig as the base skeleton of the tree's trunk because it would be strong enough to hold the massive weight of the branches as well as have enough room underneath for some type of venue.

Carved into the tree's gnarled roots, mighty trunk, and sturdy branches is a rich tapestry of 325 animals, many of which are endangered. Recently, with the extension of the roots into the Central Hub area, that number has gone up significantly, with a deer, an elephant, Rocky Mountain big horn sheep, and a bison, among others.

The first *real* tree planted at Disney's Animal Kingdom in December 1995 was an authentic Acacia xanthophlosa, grown from a seed that Disney acquired in Africa. The park has about one hundred species of real trees and shrubs foreign to North American soil.

At one point, the base of the tree was to have had the Root Restaurant, a high-class eatery at the park. Imagineer Bryan Jowers did concept artwork for a "Wonders of Nature" show to be performed there instead. Imagineer Dave Minichiello did concept artwork for a *Lion King* character show that later evolved and moved to a different area of the park.

It was CEO Michael Eisner who suggested creating an attraction inspired by the then in-production Pixar animated feature *A Bug's Life* (1998) in a 430-seat interactive theater.

The nine-minute long It's Tough to Be a Bug opened seven months before the release of the film itself. Hosted by the ant Flik from the movie, this 3D experience of film and Audio-Animatronics tries to educate the audience into accepting that insects help us and the environment.

Bits of Disneyland

Some objects from Disneyland over the years made the journey to Walt Disney World. In particular, some rather large objects came over thanks to some problems with getting Disney's Animal Kingdom ready to open in 1998.

The Animal Kingdom was meant to include areas devoted to animals real, imaginary, and extinct. Early guest surveys showed people so eager to see a dragon or a unicorn up close in the Beastly Kingdom that Disney believed that building the park was a great idea.

However, as the section of the park with "real" animals went over budget, due in part because the cost of care for and feeding the animals had been under-estimated, the Beastly Kingdom disappeared and the Imagineers, at the direction of CEO Michael Eisner, rushed to put in a temporary placeholder area.

Similar in concept to Mickey's Birthdayland at the Magic Kingdom in 1988, the Imagineers created Camp Minnie-Mickey, a summer camp set in the Adirondack Mountains of upstate New York where the Disney animated characters would go for vacation. It would be a location for meet-and-greet opportunities with the characters, but there would need to be more to fill out the space.

One of the fastest and least expensive things to add to an area is live entertainment, and it is also the easiest to remove.

Two temporary shows were created: *Pocahontas and Her Forest Friends* and *Festival of the Lion King*, that were expected to last about a year or two until the Beastly Kingdom could be revived for the second phase of the park. Both shows opened in April 1998.

However, there was a severely limited budget, so it was necessary to purchase some already built items from Disneyland that were going into storage or about to be destroyed.

For *Pocahontas and Her Forest Friends*, a large, impressive Grandmother Willow figure from Disneyland's live-action show *The*

Spirit of Pocahontas, which closed in Fall 1997, was incorporated.

While many fans think it was an expensive Audio-Animatronic prop, Grandmother Willow was actually designed to be manipulated by a puppeteer, just like the little Sprig character. The process was dubbed "Puppetronics".

In *The Festival of the Lion King*, the impressive floats that serve as intriguing set pieces are recycled from the Lion King Celebration parade that ran at Disneyland from 1994–1997. The parade featured six floats, but only four were used for *The Festival of the Lion King*.

The floats did undergo some slight modifications. For instance, the last float in the parade, Pride Rock, has Simba standing atop the rock while Nala is down below to his right at the foot of the float beating out a rhythm with her paws on the drums. Mufasa's face is represented on the spinning sun design up above.

Both Nala and Mufasa were removed from the float before it was used in the stage show.

None of these items were free. The Disney company has different business units and so these things had to be purchased by one business unit in order for the other business unit to balance its books. Shipping the items from the West Coast to the East Coast incurred expenses as well.

However, for Disneyland fans who long for a little reminder of Disneyland, this is just one example of actual bits and pieces from the Happiest Place on Earth scattered throughout the Disney World parks.

The Anandapur Reporter

The queue for Expedition Everest takes guests through the Himalayan Escapes Tours and Expeditions Booking Office to obtain "permits". This office is located in the remote village of Serka Zong in the (fictional) kingdom of Anandapur located in the foothills of the Himalayas.

The company organizes a number of different tours and expeditions, with Expedition Everest just one of them. Himalayan Escapes is operated by a native Anandapuri, Norbu, and his business partner, a British entrepreneur named Bob.

They operate out of a building that had previously been used as the headquarters of the Royal Anandapur Tea Company. They have refurbished a steam train that had been used by the tea company to bring harvested tea leaves down the mountains.

This train now takes customers to the base camp using a shortcut through the Forbidden Mountain that is supposedly the location of a mysterious environmental guardian referred to as the Yeti.

Norbu and Bob's office is filled with dozens of small details, from a map of the Himalayas to a tour board depicting the status of the various expeditions.

In fact, there are so many details in the various buildings leading to the attraction vehicles that guests are unable to see them all, including a yellowed newspaper clipping from *The Anandapur Reporter* ("Serving the Nation for 100 Years"). Headlines such as "Trekkers Feared Lost" and "Herders Report Missing Yak" are visible, but their stories are missing. The lead feature is complete:

> Forbidden Mountain Railway Re-Opens
>
> Locals Fear Wrath of Yeti
>
> SERKA ZONG—Despite dire warning from irate local residents, the old Anandapur Rail Services route through Forbidden Mountain was re-opened today. Closed since 1934 under mysterious circumstances,

the railroad, formerly operated by the Royal Anandapur Tea Co., was refurbished by Himalayan Escapes Tours and Expeditions.

The intent, say the operators, is to provide safe, efficient transport to base camp at Mount Everest and environs. Hundreds of Western trekkers and climbers are expected to make the journey to Serka Zong to book passage on the new service.

In the heyday of the great tea plantations that flourished in the region, private rail lines were established to carry produce to distant markets. The Royal Anandapur Tea Company used the Forbidden Mountain route extensively in the 1920s and early 1930s. However, beginning in 1933, the railroad was plagued with accidents. Some drew a connection between the mishaps and increasing British expeditionary attempts to reach the summit of Mount Everest, invoking the spirit of the guardian of the sacred mountain.

By 1934, continual equipment breakdowns and track breakages caused the tea company to shutter its facilities and pull up stakes. The legend of a sacred beast continued to loom large among locals, coming to a head in 1982 with the tragic disappearance of the Forbidden Mountain Expedition.

However, warnings and naysayers aside, the daring entrepreneurs behind Himalayan Escapes were determined to put on a loud, colorful show to celebrate their achievement. Local government officials in attendance trumpeted the event as a landmark enterprise, marking a new era of prosperity and opportunity for Serka Zong. It is indeed our hope that this is the case.

Near the end of the Yeti Museum, before guests board the train, two notices hang on the wall. One is written by the museum's curator, Professor Pumba Dorjay, warning against the railroad expedition, and another is by Norbu and Bob stating that the curator's notice "does not represent the opinions or views" of the company.

The Yak & Yeti

The Yak & Yeti restaurant, quick-service eatery, features Pan-Asian cuisine, but the Imagineers have given it an elaborate and intriguing back story to blend into the Asian area of Disney's Animal Kingdom.

According to the Imagineers, the restaurant is situated at the base of Mount Everest in the small village of Anandapur near a highly traveled road used by tourists, researchers, pilgrims, and traders. A wealthy merchant from Anandapur, Arjun, fell on hard times. As a result, he converted his regal home into a fine hotel and restaurant, hoping to be able to make a living from these travelers.

The original two-story stone house, painted purple, was built in June 1924. As unexpected success came to Arjun's new enterprise, he continued to expand the building haphazardly, including the addition of an authentic Indian marble pavilion on one end, and he allowed the original garden and patio to become part of the interior of the restaurant. In the lush garden adjacent to the pavilion is a collection of rare and revered lingam stones.

Arjun's success may be due, in part, to his wise placement of a statue of Ganesha, the Hindu deity known to be a "remover of obstacles" and that resembles a red elephant, in the lobby.

The hotel is a boutique establishment of the sort that wealthier adventure travelers might seek out in India. While they rest at the hotel during their journeys, the owner and other families reside there as well. Details include luggage at a check-in desk and signage for rooms and hotel guests.

The décor as well as the furniture is an amalgamation of mis-matched artifacts Arjun and his family have collected over their years of travel in Southeast Asia.

Those artifacts displayed prominently throughout Yak & Yeti are authentic and were gathered from around Southeast Asia by Schussler Creative, the group responsible for designing the location for Landry's

Restaurants. Landry's also owns and operates the Rainforest Café and T-Rex Restaurant.

The theming for Yak & Yeti is more subtle and subdued than those other restaurants, but no less effective and immersive. Since it originally was a dwelling, the dining area is spread over several small rooms rather than just occupying one large space, making it a more intimate experience.

All the work was done in association with Imagineering so that it blended with the existing mythology that had been created for the area. There are statues, ceremonial costumes, puppets, bowls, vases, antique furnishings, cabinets filled with knickknacks, and much more.

Although some items were fabricated to help tell the story, like the portrait of the current rajah and his wife that also appears elsewhere in Anandapur, including in the buildings of Himalayan Escapes Tours & Expeditions.

Pictures of the royal couple are required by law to be posted by businesses. They would be purchased from the government, making the portraits both a business license and a tax. While the couple is fictional, as is the village, the practice was real in the regions that the Imagineers studied. "Detail is there to make you believe in the reality of the story you're immersed in," said Imagineer Joe Rohde.

The restaurant opened November 14, 2007, and is the only non-Disney restaurant inside the park.

Landry's general manager, Marty Sherman, said:

> The sights, sounds, and energy of this novel dining destination will transport guests to another culture. The moment diners arrive at Yak & Yeti, they will feel like they've stepped into an authentic Himalayan village. It is a place to immerse yourself in a culture that is mysterious, exotic, and exciting.

Chester and Hester

Perhaps one of the most misunderstood stories at the parks is the tale of Chester and Hester and their dinosaur store and amusement venue in DinoLand. It is its own little mini-Jurassic world.

In the 1940s, Diggs County, now the home of the Dino Institute, was a quiet rural location with just a few cabins and a fishing lodge. Newly married Chester and Hester, who grew up in the area, decided to open a business, since they reasoned that there would be an influx of traffic with Route 498 (April 98, or 4/98, was when Disney's Animal Kingdom opened) becoming part of the fabled Route 66.

They put their life savings into building a service station. Since they were the only stop for gasoline for miles, they had made a wise investment.

However, in 1947, amateur paleontologists discovered a fossil, and it was speculated that the area might be rife with even more fossils of scientific interest.

The group bought the lodge and turned it into the first Dino Institute. Eventually, they grew so large they moved into a new building in April 1978, and now the place is inhabited by college students who use it both as a dormitory and a commissary.

Chester and Hester even found some fossils themselves after digging in their backyard and sold them to passing tourists. It proved so popular that the couple began selling more and more dinosaur-related souvenirs, and found they made more money from that endeavor with less effort than selling gas. So the establishment evolved into Chester and Hester's Dinosaur Treasures.

Since the couple didn't have enough money to start over fresh, they repainted many of the things from the gas station. They still have cans of oil, fan belts, and other automotive items that they continue to sell.

A photo of the couple in their twilight years is in the shop, and sharp-eyed guests can see that they look almost exactly alike, as if the same person posed for both characters.

Then the Dino Institute discovered time travel, and there was a flood of people coming to participate. Chester and Hester took over the cracked parking lot across the street and turned it into a small roadside attraction, similar to those popular along the real Route 66.

Classic Roadside Attractions featured statues, mini-museums, quirky architecture, gimmicky signage, and unique exhibits designed to separate a curious tourist from the money in his wallet. Many of those attractions included massive cement dinosaurs.

Chester and Hester's Dino-Rama proclaimed: "Dinosaurs the way they were meant to be: big, green and fun!" They opened their amusement park 2002. (Interestingly, on I-4 between Tampa and Orlando you'll find Dinosaur World, which opened in 1998 and billed itself as the largest dinosaur attraction in the world, with over two hundred life-sized dinosaurs in native vegetation.)

Of course, money was tight for such a major investment, so Chester and Hester had to purchase "off-the-shelf" amusement rides and carnival games that have been re-themed to dinosaurs. These are not rides of distinction, but "rides of extinction", as one highly colorful sign states.

To compete with the Dino Institute's technological achievement, Chester and Hester offered guests a trip on Primeval Whirl, which also sends guests back in time where at the end of their journey the confront an asteroid.

The name of this wild mouse ride is an homage to the Primeval World, Ford Motor Company's pavilion at the 1964 New York World's Fair that featured full-sized Audio-Animatronic dinosaurs designed by Disney and later installed as the grand finale of the Disneyland Railroad.

PART TWO

The Walt Disney World Resorts

Walt Disney World offers guests many opportunities to stay on Disney property. (The date that each resort was opened is given in parentheses.)

Deluxe

- Animal Kingdom Lodge (April 16, 2001)
- Beach Club (November 19, 1990)
- Boardwalk Inn (July 1, 1996)
- Contemporary (October 1, 1971)
- Grand Floridian Resort & Spa (July 1, 1988)
- Polynesian Village Resort (October 1, 1971)
- Wilderness Lodge (May 28,1994)
- Yacht Club (November 5 1990)

Moderate

- Caribbean Beach (October 1, 1988)
- Coronado Springs (August 1, 1997)
- Port Orleans: French Quarter (May 17, 1991)
- Port Orleans: Riverside (February 2, 1992) formerly Dixie Landings

Value

- All-Star Movies (January 15, 1999)
- All-Star Music (November 22, 1994)

- All-Star Sports (April 24, 1994)
- Art of Animation (May 21, 2012)
- Pop Century (December 14, 2003)

Other

- Fort Wilderness Resort and Campground (November 19, 1974)
- Shades of Green (February 1, 1994) is owned by the U.S. Department of Defense. Originally, it was a WDW resort named Disney's Golf Resort (1973) and then the Disney Inn (1986). Disney still owns the land that the resort is on.
- Walt Disney World Swan (January 13, 1990) is owned by the Tishman Hotel Corporation, but operated by Starwood Hotels & Resorts Worldwilde under the Westin Hotels brand.
- Walt Disney World Dolphin (June 1, 1990) is owned by the Tishman Hotel Corporation, but operated by Starwood Hotels & Resorts Worldwilde under the Sheraton Hotels brand.
- There are nine Disney Vacation Club resort facilities on property.

Training for the WDW Resorts

Walt's parents, Elias and Flora Disney, actually lived in the central Florida area. They were married there in Kismet (a town that no longer exists) in January 1888. That same year, they managed the Hallifax Hotel in Daytona Beach.

That hotel no longer exists either, although there is still a Hallifax Avenue where the Hallifax Hotel once stood. When attendance dropped off significantly in the fall, after all the tourists had left, the Disney family could not make a living with the hotel, and so they moved to Chicago.

Decades later, there were still not many hotels in central Florida, for the same reason.

Orlando attorney Finley Hamilton dabbled in real estate. He had opened a Hilton Inn on Colonial Drive and then acquired ten acres on Sand Lake Road near an I-4 ramp to build the Hilton Inn South.

The two story, horseshoe-shaped hotel had 140 guest rooms and a covered pool as well as several meeting rooms. People called it "Finley's Folly", but Hamilton was counting on it developing into a visible and accessible stop for visitors to Walt Disney World.

Because it was so near Disney property, the Disney company offered to manage it for Hamilton for sixteen months, until Walt Disney World opened, so they could train their staff for the Contemporary and Polynesian resorts.

Hamilton and his partner paved the nearby dirt road. Hamilton wanted to call it "Hamilton Drive", but there was another street by that name in Orlando so he had to settle for "International Drive".

When the Disney company determined they would run the WDW resort hotels themselves, Disney executive John Curry was put in charge and he hired a half-dozen managers from Western International who were originally going to run the Polynesian. Marriott was to have handled the Contemporary.

Dan Darrow was brought in from the Sheraton as general manager. Bill "Sully" Sullivan was made the assistant manager, primarily to teach the Disney way of doing things to the hotel employees.

Although it had been open since 1968, the Hilton Inn South re-opened May 1970 under Disney management and was the location where Disney executives stayed, as well as Disney transfers who had not yet found a permanent home in the area. It was also open to the general public, but the standards were extremely high because Roy O. Disney himself visited frequently and commented on flaws.

Oddly, even though he was an attorney, Hamilton trusted the Disney company and the running of the Hilton Inn South was just a "handshake" deal.

Hamilton claimed in a letter to Disney President Donn Tatum that he suffered an estimated loss of over $50,000 in revenue during the time Disney managed the hotel. Hamilton never collected nor sued because he felt that Disney would be a great source of business and he was in the process of building yet another hotel. The Hilton Inn South no longer exists, but it was originally in the same general area as the big McDonald's and the entrance to the Quality Inn on Sand Lake Road.

Former Disney Archivist Dave Smith recalled:

> To train the cast members who were going to manage our hotels, we leased the Hilton Inn South, on International Drive near Sand Lake Road. At least I assume it was a lease—I have never seen the actual documents. I stayed there on my first trip to Orlando, in June 1971. They put up most of the traveling Disney executives there, but, of course, at that time there were few other choices nearby.

Humphrey the Bear

Disney's Wilderness Lodge is the only Disney resort hotel to have an official mascot, the brown bear. Images and allusions to it can be found throughout the resort, including bear tracks embedded in the walkways.

To make that potentially fearsome mascot more friendly for younger guests, some of the brown bear images are of the Disney animated character Humphrey, a lovable, overweight brown bear who lives in the fictional Brownstone National Park.

Humphrey is most prominent on a totem pole on the outside of the Mercantile Store in the lobby of the resort that was carved out of cedar by William Robertson. A smiling Humphrey is at the bottom of the pole supporting frontier-garbed Mickey Mouse, Goofy, and Donald Duck above him. Over the years, the store has sold exclusive merchandise featuring the image of Humphrey.

In addition, Humphrey pops up on signage throughout the resort that many guests fail to notice. On the road leading to the Wilderness Lodge, just to right before the archway, is a round metal sign with silhouettes of Mickey Mouse being followed by Humphrey.

At the entrance to the Villas at Wilderness Lodge is another metal sign with the silhouettes of Mickey walking along and Humphrey riding on top of an old-fashioned penny farthing bicycle to mark the bike crossing path.

Only seven Disney cartoon characters have starred in their own theatrical cartoon series. Humphrey the Bear was the last one to do so before Disney decided to stop making theatrical cartoon shorts.

Humphrey starred prominently in four Donald Duck cartoons, *Rugged Bear* (1953), *Grin and Bear It* (1954), *Bearly Asleep* (1955), and *Beezy Bear* (1955). He was so popular that Disney gave him his own series, but only two cartoons were completed, *Hooked Bear* (1956) and *In the Bag* (1956).

In addition, Humphrey appeared in the opening credits for the original *Mickey Mouse Club* television series in 1955 holding the trampoline on which various characters bounce Mickey high into the air.

Humphrey the Bear does not speak, but communicates through expressive grunts supplied by voice man Jimmy MacDonald who also did the voice of Mickey Mouse. Sometimes, director Jack Hannah would step in to supply some of the grunts.

Hannah directed all the Humphrey the Bear animated appearances in the Golden Age of Disney animation. He revealed:

> For the sake of something new, we tried the Duck with a bear and it seemed like an immediate success for them to play against each other. Later, when we started thinking of another picture for the Bear, it seemed natural to be in a national forest, and that's how the Little Ranger came into being. The Little Ranger always treated his bears like his own pets, and I always found that funny, as did the audience.

Humphrey has also appeared in cartoons made for television, including those on the House of Mouse and Mickey Mouse Clubhouse shows. He even has a short cameo at the end of the film *Who Framed Roger Rabbit* (1988).

While Humphrey never appeared in any cartoon featuring him in the circus, he was recently revived to be included in the New Fantasyland expansion. He is prominent on the sign for Big Top Treats "Circus Snacks Galore" with him happily munching away on a caramel apple. In addition, that same image is used on a Storybook Circus poster.

However, while he may sneak over to the Magic Kingdom to grab a tasty treat, his official Walt Disney World home is Wilderness Lodge.

Grand Canyon Fireplace

Visiting the lobby of the Wilderness Lodge Resort, Walt Disney World guests can glimpse over 1.6 billion years of history depicted on the majestic fireplace in the corner.

The Bright Angel Lodge at the Grand Canyon has a small geologic fireplace that was quarried directly from the layers of the Grand Canyon, but the Imagineers went for a more dramatic storytelling version for the Wilderness Lodge.

The fireplace is an intricate 82-foot-high replica of the South Rim Grand Canyon strata. As you ascend the levels of the lobby, you travel upward to modern times. To see evidence of the first creatures to squirm over and under the surface of the earth, guests should go to the fourth floor and search the layers of Tapeats Sandstone for worm borrows and trilobite trails.

Paleontologist (and artist) Robert Reid was sent to study the actual walls of the Grand Canyon.

His studies were reproduced in a detailed book that was used to help contractors create the fireplace, replete with a kaleidoscope of colors, rocks, and fossils—many of which are real.

Some of the fossils of prehistoric plant and animal life are several hundred millions years old and are carefully embedded in the correct stratus for a historically accurate view. They pre-date the dinosaur era.

Over 100 colors in hues of green, magenta, buff, red, black, and brown are visible. From the Vishnu Schist to Bass Limestone to Tapeats Sandstone to the Redwall and Temple Butte Limestone and finally ending with Kaibab Limestone and Toroweap Formation, the fireplace represents the 1.6 billion years it took for the layers of rock to form.

The variations are re-created in the same proportions as those that appear in the real Grand Canyon that range from 50–700 feet thick.

The fireplace is built to scale with the geologic layout of the Grand Canyon, complete with geologic disconformities (periods of deposition, erosion, tilting, and renewed deposition on top of the older rocks). The detail is nearly perfect, with the textbook diagrams documenting the geology of the Grand Canyon.

Samples of elements from each strata are housed in glass display cases near the fireplace on each floor level. These displays describe the epoch that particular section of the fireplace rock represents.

One of the things that does not exist in the real Grand Canyon is a Hidden Mickey, but it does in the Wilderness Lodge fireplace.

Directly facing the fireplace, on the right-hand side of the three-sided fireplace where a lodge pole is jutting out before the next floor, you'll find the famous three-circled Mickey Mouse head in the reddish rock.

At the Guest Services front desk, guests can get a riddle clue sheet to help them locate the over two dozen other Hidden Mickeys at the Wilderness Lodge.

The Wilderness Lodge fireplace is a real working fireplace. Originally, it burned wood, which caused several challenges over the early years, such as raising the humidity level in the lobby which caused the wood used in the massive cedar totem poles to crack.

It was converted to a gas-burning fireplace for a number of reasons, including the fact that gas is safer and can be more easily controlled than an open flame.

The Story Behind the Story

Disney's Saratoga Springs Resort and Spa opened on May 17, 2004, with a "health-history-horses" theme. The development manager for the project was Kevin Cummings.

Cummings was born and raised in Saratoga Springs, New York, the city that was the inspiration for this Disney Vacation Club resort. In fact, at the time, his twin brother still lived in that historic upstate New York town so Cummings would go back to visit several times during the year.

In his role as a development manager, Cummings oversaw the hiring of the project's design professionals, from the design architect to the working architect to all the engineers. "I coordinate them as a team to come up with the design for our project," he stated.

As soon as Cummings heard that the new resort was to be inspired by the tranquil towns of upstate New York in the 1800s, he said:

> It's got to be Saratoga! We took trips up there to look at the architecture, and I'd show my friends around since I knew the lay of the land. I knew exactly where to look, where the best architecture was—North Broadway, Union Avenue, and all the special buildings that we took bits and pieces of our design from for the resort.

Working with Boston-based Graham Gund Architects (who had worked on Disney's Vero Beach Resort, the Celebration Hotel in Celebration, Florida, and Disney's Coronado Springs Resort), the team, according to Cummings:

> [W]ent up and down the East Coast looking for different elements to be put to use for our buildings. Of course, the major part of the architecture is based on Saratoga. But we were very careful to use actual design elements—it's really real, what you're seeing, we didn't make this stuff up.

> Of course, I knew the history from growing up and going to school there, the local history, and the history of the racecourse. It's *not*

a racetrack—it's a racecourse—the oldest racecourse in the United States, going all the way back to 1863. In the 1920s and 1930s, especially, Saratoga was the place for the upper class to summer, and they all went during the racing season. It was known as the "August place". Saratoga Springs used to have more hotel rooms than any other U.S. destination.

Cummings helped develop a binder filled with photos from the research trips so that the smallest details like the awnings would be accurate.

He was also instrumental in naming many of the features like the High Rock Spring Pool after one of the actual "healing springs" found in the city and frequented by celebrities and even U.S. presidents.

Street names such as Union Avenue and Broadway will also be familiar to people who know Saratoga Springs. Cummings wanted to see the name of the street he grew up on included, but it didn't make the cut.

What most reminded him of his hometown, however, were the three towers. He said:

> We have three different building types, and we have three different tower designs on the guest room buildings.
>
> They're right at the entrances, and they rise 70 feet into the air—those elements really strike you. You'll see them all over Saratoga, even the colors. The blues, greens, reds, and yellows we used to paint the buildings—the greatest homes in Saratoga Springs have those colors. That's what really hit me—the colors of the buildings...and the towers. No doubt about it.

The elegant train station at the Magic Kingdom was built to resemble a similar turn-of-the-century train station in Saratoga, New York.

The Story Behind the Story

Disney's Dixie Landings Resort opened on February 2, 1992, themed to the Antebellum South of steamboat travel, formal garden parties, and mint juleps on the front porch. It was inspired by rural Louisiana and nestled alongside the picturesque Sassagoula River (the Native American term for the Mississippi).

In 2001, to eliminate the negative connotations associated with the Old South, including a cotton mill that suggested the slavery of the pre-Civil War era as well as the word "Dixie", the resort was merged into Disney's Port Orleans resort to become Port Orleans Riverside.

Riverside is divided into two distinctly themed parishes: the stately white-columned Magnolia Bend "mansions" reminiscent of the Old South and the quaint backwoods "cottages" of Alligator Bayou themed after Cajun Country.

When it first opened, Disney's Port Orleans Resort had a faux newspaper called *The Sassagoula Sentinel* referring to the man-made river that flowed outside. When Dixie Landings opened about a year later, it also had a newspaper, *The Sassagoula Times* (supposedly originally printed in 1893 and costing five cents, but given free to guests).

These newspapers provided guest information, but were also filled with stories that were a mixture of authentic history mixed with fanciful but logical additions from Imagineering.

Today, resort guests receive a generic Directory of Services and Resort Map, a small pocket-sized pamphlet containing just the basic service information, but no background story or fun facts.

According to stories in the original issue of *The Sassagoula Times*, Dixie Landings was founded by a pair of brothers from Port Orleans. Colonel J.C. Peace and his brother Everette came up river to make their own home away from the hustle and bustle of the city.

Everette, the recluse of the family who often spent days on end whittling small carvings with a remarkable degree of detail, settled on a remote island in 1835 in the heart of what later became known as Alligator Bayou, to live the life of a hermit. Legends arose about this Old Man Island and its odd inhabitant.

Everette's younger brother, Jonathon, who was an honorary colonel like Colonel Sanders of KFC fame, was much more outgoing. He constructed a stately home known as Acadian House. Neighbors would pay visits on one another regularly, the cotton trade brought numerous business guests, and steamboats along the vital Sassagoula accounted for a steady stream of visitors from across the country.

Before long, a community of stately Southern mansions arose in this tranquil part of the Sassagoula, commonly called Magnolia Bend.

Over the years, Jonathon had heard tall tales of the mysterious Old Man living on Old Man Island but dismissed them as legend. One day, his granddaughter, Susie, came running to him with a beautifully carved wooden bird in her hand. She told stories of the funny old man who had given it to her.

Turning over the rustic treasure, he could barely make out the tiny letters carved into the base: "Everette Peace, 1857".

Immediately, the colonel made his way out to the island loudly shouting his older brother's name. The two embraced warmly. Despite Jonathon's offer to come live with him, Everette had no desire to leave his little island. Jonathon continued to visit his brother many nights to reminisce, until their deaths.

That back story has been long forgotten today.

The Story Behind the Story

The Polynesian Village Resort opened along with the Magic Kingdom and the Contemporary Resort on October 1, 1971, but was renamed Disney's Polynesian Resort in 1985. It reverted to its original name in 2014.

The resort was meant to be an homage to Tiki culture, an American interpretation of Polynesian culture primarily reflected in West Coast restaurants like Don the Beachcomber and Trader Vic's that started appearing after World War II to rekindle fond memories for military personnel who had served in the South Pacific.

Originally, the resort was to look like a triangular island volcano twelve stories high with a South Seas restaurant at the top. Surrounding this main building would be smaller longhouses to accommodate guests.

That design was later modified by the architectural firm of Welton Becket and Associates into the current three-story structure of a smaller main building known as the Great Ceremonial House (modeled after a Tahitian royal assembly lodge) and more longhouses to include the additional guest rooms that were to be in the original massive building.

The back of the resort's original postcard stated:

> A tropical island adventure awaits guests at the Polynesian Village Resort. Entertainment, food, décor, and shopping all blend into a South Seas vacation atmosphere. Palm-lined sandy beaches are just a barefoot stroll away, while the "rest of the World" is reached by outrigger, sailboats, old-fashioned side-wheel steamboats, and swift monorail trains.

The resort opened with 492 guest rooms in eight longhouse buildings: Bali Hai, Bora Bora, Hawaii, Fiji, Samoa, Tahiti, Tonga, and Maui. Resort rates in 1971 were $29 to $44 a night, depending on several factors, including the floor, view, and location.

At a facility on the upper east end of WDW property roughly four miles away from the resort, U.S. Steel workers produced hundreds of modular rooms weighing 8.5 tons each that were finished and furnished in an assembly-line process for both the Contemporary and the Polynesian. The building where all of that work took place still stands at 1500 Live Oak Lane, just south of the softball field.

The Polynesian rooms were stacked rather than slid into place like at the Contemporary's A-frame structure, but the basic process of construction of the individual rooms was similar. For decorative purposes, real bamboo had been used in the resort, but it quickly split and rotted, forcing a last-minute replacement of fiberglass bamboo in many areas.

At first, elaborate luaus were held on an outdoor stage on the beach, but the unpredictable Florida weather caused so many cancellations that in 1972 the sheltered Luau Cove was constructed to house the festivities.

The pool at the resort in 1971 was the Nanea Volcano Pool, where guests had to go under a waterfall to get to the stairs to reach the top of the water slide. That pool was replaced in March 2001 with the current pool featuring a larger volcano.

The resort saw two major rehabs in 1978 and 1985, with the addition of more buildings and the renaming of some existing structures.

In 1999, most of the resort's longhouses were renamed to more accurately reflect the Polynesian islands: Bali Hai became Tonga, Bora Bora became Niue, Hawaii became Samoa, Maori changed to Rarotonga;, Moorea became Tahiti, Oahu became Tokelau, Pago Pago became Rapa Nui, Samoa became Tuvalu, Tahiti became Aotearoa, and Tonga became Hawaii.

The names were changed to better reflect a more accurate geographical position of the islands to each other.

A recent renovation in 2014 resulted in the disappearance of the massive lobby waterfall and the addition of the DVC Bora Bora Bungalows.

Mutoscopes

Located in the Disney BoardWalk Inn and Villas resort hallway directly across from the restrooms near the Belle Vue Lounge are green and red clamshell Mutoscopes. At one time, there was also a Mutoscope that was painted white with gold trim.

Mutoscopes were originally manufactured from 1895 to 1909 by the American Mutoscope and Biograph Company.

The red and green Mutoscopes are authentic operating machines from this time period, and you can still clearly see the appropriate markings on the front of the machines.

The cast iron clamshell was one of the most durable styles and is so named because of the clamshell design pattern on both sides.

Mutoscopes were basically a huge mechanical "flip book" with about 850 sturdy photographic prints on individual cards attached to a central core and flipped by a hand-cranked ratchet.

Each coin-operated machine only had a single reel, often an excerpt from an existing silent film, but sometimes an original, and lasting about a minute.

The patron could control the presentation speed, but only to a limited degree. The crank could be turned in both directions, although this did not reverse the playing of the reel. Nor could the patron extend viewing time by stopping the crank, because the flexible images were bent into the proper viewing position by tension applied from forward cranking.

Stopping the crank reduced the forward tension on the reels, causing the reel to go backwards and the picture to move from the viewing position; a spring in the mechanism turned off the light and in some models brought down a shutter which completely blocked out the picture.

For the opening of Walt Disney World, the Disney company bought a large collection of authentic mutoscopes, mechanical games, and

Orchestrions (music boxes like "Big Bertha" at Disney's Grand Floridian Resort and Spa) from Paul Eakin in the 1970s and moved them all from where they were being displayed and stored in Missouri to Florida. (Some machines from the Disneyland collection were also shipped out to Florida.)

Eakin's collection of machines operated for many years at the Million Dollar Museum in Sikeston and the Gay 90s Melody Museum in St. Louis. Both Missouri museums were closed when Eakin sold the bulk of his collection to Walt Disney World.

These two particular mutoscopes were part of that collection and were enjoyed by Disney guests at the Main Street Penny Arcade until it closed March 19, 1995, to become part of the Main Street Athletic Company.

A handful of the machines were eventually moved to the upper floor of the Main Street Train Station while the rest were stored under Cinderella Castle in a small, leaky room in the Utilidors. Most of the collection is no longer in storage, but was sold off to private collectors in 1997.

The red and green machines were rescued from under the Magic Kingdom in 1996 and installed in one of the animation classrooms at the Disney Institute, where they were used as an enhancement for an animation history class.

When the Disney Institute stopped offering individual programs to guests in 2000, and then later left the physical space altogether in 2002, the Mutoscopes found a new home at the BoardWalk Inn where a little tender loving care may help them spring back to life to continue to delight guests.

Luna Park References

The BoardWalk Inn and Villas was designed to incorporate aspects of the iconic Atlantic City Boardwalk and the fabled Coney Island playground to create an East Coast seaside vacation destination from the early 1900s.

Luna Park Pool is a reference to one of the most popular early amusement parks at Coney Island. Luna Park was built and operated by Frederic Thompson and Elmer "Skip" Dundy from 1903–1944. It was one of three major entertainment parks at Coney Island, and included Steeplechase Park and Dreamland.

That's the reason why the proprietor of the On the Boardwalk Thimbles & Threads shop is F. Thompson, and inside the resort's main lobby is Dundy's Sundries—Serving the Boadwalk since 1902.

It is 1902 because Thompson and Dundy's amazing ride from the 1901 Pan-American Exposition (the name of the World's Fair held in New York) called A Trip to the Moon was moved to Coney Island's Steeplechase Park for the 1902 season.

It was an electrically powered dark ride where thirty passengers boarded a wooden spacecraft and were taken on a visit to the moon complete with little people dressed up as moon men. The ride proved so popular that Thompson and Dundy earned enough money to build their own amusement venue, Luna Park.

"Luna" is Latin for "moon" (and also the name of the airship vehicle in their attraction). Dundy's sister was also named Luna.

Why are there elephants at the pool?

One of the biggest attractions at Coney Island's Luna Park was its private herd of elephants, which roamed freely. Elephant rides were popular for the guests as well as a once-in-a-lifetime experience.

However, cleaning an elephant is a long, arduous task, so it was quickly discovered that taking the elephants out to the Atlantic Ocean to bathe was not only easier, but it was free publicity for the park.

The Keister Coaster is meant to be reminiscent of the many classic wooden roller coasters at Coney Island in its prime. That's why it is a seemingly wooden structure.

However, the huge clown face at the end is not just to reference the many clowns at Coney Island, one of whom was the famous animation director Dave Fleischer who was rotoscoped in his clown outfit to become KoKo the Clown, the famous silent animated cartoon character.

One of the popular midway games was the Clown Water Gun Balloon Game where a patron would shoot water into the open mouth of the head of a clown to build up pressure to inflate the balloon on the head to pop first, and thus defeat other players competing to do the exact same thing with other clown heads.

The game still exists today and is popular. A variation of the game, an auto race, is one of the midway games in the Wildwood Landing section on Disney's boardwalk.

The nearby Ferris W. Eahlers Community Hall is not an obscure reference to a turn-of-the-century personality or an Imagineer. Said aloud it sounds like "Ferris Wheelers", a reference to the Coney Island Ferris wheels.

While most guests are unfamiliar with these connections, for those few who are it enhances an already premium experience.

The Dragon Calliope

For the 1955 Mickey Mouse Club Circus Parade at Disneyland, Walt Disney purchased some authentic turn-of-the-century circus wagons and had them carefully restored. In fact, anything removed from a wagon during the restoration, Walt preserved.

He purchased nine authentic circus wagons from Dave Bradley who was using them as decorations outside the entrance to his kiddie park, the Beverly Park Amusement Center, at the corner of Beverly and La Cienga in Los Angeles where Walt would take his young daughters on Sunday outings.

In this purchase was a 1907 twenty-whistle steam calliope that was in disrepair.

Its first appearance was in the Mugivan and Bowers shows in England, circa 1907, after which it was sold to Ken Maynard's Diamond K Circus in 1936. At a cost of $50,000, Disney redesigned the calliope to resemble the others in the collection, and adorned its wagon with decorative pieces from some of Disney's other circus wagons, transforming it into the Dragon Calliope.

Take a close look at the calliope car behind the engine of Disneyland's Casey Jr. train. The dragon is an exact re-creation of the one on the calliope, since it is a circus train.

Many of the circus wagons, as well as the calliope, appear in the Disney live-action film, *Toby Tyler, or Ten Weeks with a Circus* (1960). Starring young Kevin Corcoran and based on the novel of the same name by James Otis Kaler, the film recounts a young boy running away to work in a circus and becoming a circus star after befriending a mischievous chimp.

The film's world premiere was held January 21, 1960, at the Florida Theater in Sarasota, Florida, the winter home of the Ringling Brothers and Barnum & Bailey Circus (now owned and operated by Feld Entertainment, who produce the Disney on Ice shows).

Just as the parade and the opening credits are ending, the Dragon Calliope comes in to view, followed by the eager Toby Tyler, as music and steam billow from the colorful wagon.

In 1962, Walt would donate the wagons (including the pieces that had been removed) to the Circus World Museum in Baraboo, Wisconsin, where they are taken care of and displayed to this day. However, he kept the Dragon Calliope.

Besides being part of the short-lived Mickey Mouse Club Circus Parade, the calliope went on to appear in many Disneyland parades through the park's 25th anniversary.

It was repainted silver and blue and pulled by six black Percheron horses the following year when it was relocated to Florida for the Walt Disney World Tencennial celebration in 1981. Since then, it was seen in numerous parades at Walt Disney World, including several Christmas broadcasts, until it was retired from parade duty.

The last time the Dragon Calliope was used publicly was January 2, 2007, in Tallahassee, Florida, where Mickey and Minnie Mouse were participants in the inaugural parade for newly sworn-in governor, Charlie Crist. Mickey and Minnie in the calliope were pulled by a team of eight black Percheron horses.

The Tri-Circle-D Ranch at the Fort Wilderness Resort and Campground at Walt Disney World is now the home for the famous Dragon Calliope. It can be viewed by guests and it is free to do so. It is even rigged so that by pushing a button, it briefly plays a tune.

The calliope is located near another free hidden treasure, a small exhibit named Walt Disney Horses dedicated to Walt's love of horses and to the different roles horses perform at Walt Disney World.

River Country

River Country! Big River Country.
It's a hoot. It's a holler! It's a water jamboree!
River Country. Big River Country.
If you're hot around the collar, it's the cool place to be!

That is the opening verse of a 1977 song written about a forgotten Walt Disney World popular attraction.

Walt Disney World defined the concept of a themed water park with the opening of Disney's River Country on June 20, 1976, as part of the Fort Wilderness Resort on the shore of Bay Lake.

Originally, this water park was going to be called Pop's Willow Grove and was meant to be reminiscent of an "old fishing hole" from the time period of Tom Sawyer and Huck Finn, with items like rope swings enhancing that story.

River Country was about one-fourth the size of Typhoon Lagoon, since the Disney company had no idea whether such a then-radical idea would be successful.

Attractions included a 330,000 gallon clear-water pool called Upstream Plunge; Slippery Slide Falls; two sixteen-foot rock slides with faux rock work (scattered with pebbles from stream beds in Georgia and the Carolinas) created by Imagineer Fred Joerger, who did rock work on everything from the Jungle Cruise's Schweitzer Falls to Big Thunder Mountain; and the Ol' Swimmin' Hole, that was dedicated by President Gerald Ford's daughter, Susan.

The Ol' Swimmin' Hole had Whoop-n-Holler Hollow featuring two long winding chutes that ended with a splashing entry into the water.

Water from nearby Bay Lake was pumped through the inside of River Country's artificial mountain to the top of the flumes and raft ride at the rate of 8,500 gallons a minute, and then through the miracle of gravity eventually spilled back into the lake.

There was a natural soft sand beach underfoot the massive pool rather than a concrete bottom, which was a unique innovation at the time.

Even with the filtration system, the water from the lake was not completely purified and that caused some red flags for Disney Legal.

River Country's popularity resulted in many sold-out days, since the water park had limited capacity. It became apparent that a larger water park was needed, but it took just over a decade for it to become a reality.

Typhoon Lagoon opened on June 1, 1989, just across the street from the newly built Pleasure Island, and was home to the world's largest outdoor surf pool (not just a wave pool). That new water park also proved popular, so in 1995, Blizzard Beach was opened to accommodate the demand.

These new options led to a drop in attendance at the more difficult-to-access River Country. In 1998, the water park tried to compete with the "All-American Water Party" promotion where every day was celebrated as the Fourth of July, with games, Disney characters in country costumes, live country music, and good old-fashioned barbeque.

In September 2001, River Country quietly closed at the end of the summer season and never re-opened. In 2002, Walt Disney World spokesman Bill Warren told *The Orlando Sentinel* that River Country could be re-opened if "there's enough guest demand".

Supposedly, River Country could not claim the honor of being America's first water park (a designation given to Wet 'n Wild, which opened in 1977), because it was considered not a separate park, but an extension of the resort.

Even today, over a decade later, the decaying ruins of the innovative water park remain, but are hidden behind walls and are off-limits to current Disney guests.

Scales the Sea Serpent

The text on the back of the very first postcard released for the Port Orleans Resort in May 1991 stated:

> Evoking a bygone era of romance and charm, the hidden courtyards, splashing fountains, and lush gardens of Disney's Port Orleans Resort create a welcome retreat. At the heart of it all is Doubloon Lagoon, where "Scales" the sea serpent invites visitors to make a splash!

Scales was an original Disney character created for the resort. His name was coined by Disney writer Greg Ehrbar, who was working for Walt Disney World marketing and who also named other locations like Doubloon Lagoon, after the coins thrown to guests at Madri Gras.

Contrary to popular belief, the sea serpent's name was not originally meant to be a direct reference to the fact that he had scales like a dragon or a fish.

Port Orleans once had a full-service restaurant called Bonfamille's Cafe and next to it was Scat Cat's Club. Disney animation fans will instantly remember that retired opera singer Madame Bonfamille was the owner of the talented French cats in the animated feature *The Aristocats* (1970). Those famous felines were assisted in their adventures by a jazz band of cats led by their outrageous leader, Scat Cat.

There was a special children's menu for Bonfamille's Cafe, written by Ehrbar and illustrated by Peter Emslie. In the form of a photo album journal by Madame Adelaide Bonfamille, the booklet described how the good madame, Duchess, the kittens, Thomas O'Malley, and the Alley Cat Band took a musical cruise vacation from Paris to New Orleans, where they were "tailed" (followed) by a jazz-loving sea serpent.

The sea creature fell in love with the jazz that Scat Cat and his band played during the voyage. Ehrbar is a well-respected Disney musicologist with two books on the subject and so he named the serpent Scales in a nod to musical scales and the Sherman Brothers' tune from the film, "Scales and Arpeggios".

The story closes with Scales staying at the resort to enjoy the music played by the resident "jazz gators". That's why the costumed alligator statues with musical instruments are walking down the path to the pool. Just like pied pipers, they lead Scales to the pool just as they do guests today.

When the resort first opened, guests received a copy of the *Sassagoula Sentinel*, a faux newspaper that included guest information along with a fictional back story for the resort.

While Disney Imagineers loved the name that Ehrbar had come up with for the sea serpent, they wanted a story that was more in tune with the rest of the back story they had created for the resort.

In their version, in order to frighten their children from exploring the swampy marshes and the dangers like alligators and snakes, the first settlers came up with the legend of a large serpentine creature that lurks beneath the surface of the still waters waiting to gobble up unsuspecting children.

When some of the older children did not believe the myth, a group of fathers decided to teach them a lesson and constructed a large dragon-like serpent out of fence wire and bed sheets to scare them. Over the years, the serpent became a fixture of the Mardi Gras parades and was honored with his own water slide in the lagoon.

Whichever version of the story you chose to believe, it is just another example of how Walt Disney World resorts are filled with hidden storytelling treasures.

The Myth of Removable Rooms

A decades-old Disney urban myth still believed by many WDW cast members and guests is that the Contemporary Resort was designed so that the individual rooms were created like dresser drawers that could be easily slid into the framework and then later unplugged to refurnish the rooms with improvements.

The final design for the Contemporary was a collaboration between Walt Disney Productions, the United States Steel Corporation, and Los Angeles architect Welton Becket, a long-time friend of Walt Disney. There was never any documentation or publicity from any of these organizations about removable rooms.

Walt's original concept for the Epcot project was that the 20,000 residents wouldn't own their apartments and houses, and that would allow various companies from American industry to come in every five or ten years and re-do the entire kitchen or the wiring so it would feature the latest technology to showcase to visitors. This idea may have been the beginning of the urban myth of the replaceable rooms at the Contemporary.

Actually, the exterior design of the Contemporary was inspired by a building in Walt's original model for Epcot that would have been a shopping center between the center of the city and the green belt.

Walt was always fascinated by new construction methods even as far back as the Monsanto House of the Future at Disneyland, which was made from nearly indestructible plastic. United States Steel Corporation, through its then newly-formed subsidiary company, U.S. Steel Realty Development, was eager to use and publicize a unique construction method called "unitized modular construction".

For the Contemporary, they built a superstructure of thirteen steel-trussed A-frames resembling a skeletal honeycomb. Into the honeycomb they fitted the individual guest rooms manufactured at a 150,000-square-foot building just a few miles away from the resort.

The rooms were formed on an assembly line, much like automobiles, at the rate of about forty a week. As they passed through each station on the way to completion, the electrical, mechanical, and plumbing facilities were added to the room.

Each room was nine feet high, fifteen feet wide and about thirty feet long, and had air conditioning units, piping, lighting, and even mirrors and bath fixtures. Then each nine-ton room was placed on a truck and hauled to the Contemporary, where it was lifted into place by massive cranes and fitted into the steel frame.

They often didn't fit into those exact openings on the first try, and because of the structure, they had to alternate installing rooms on the opposite sides to prevent the framework from becoming off-balance and tipping over—a problem that would have occurred if a number of rooms were removed at the same time.

Once the rooms were in place and hooked up, they "settled" thanks to movement in the building, gravity, and other factors, sinking to just below their original slot. To be removed, among many other challenges, they would have to be lifted up before being pulled out.

The rooms were permanently enclosed in the structure by exterior walls and balconies. When it's time to replace the wallpaper in the rooms, it makes much more sense to send in a few wallpaper hangers than to remove the exterior walls of the Contemporary, lease an expensive crane, bring in a highly skilled crane crew, disconnect all utilities including sewer connections, carefully remove the rooms (each time leaving a hole in the side of the building), swap out the room, reconnect everything, and rebuild the exterior walls and balconies.

PART THREE

The Rest of
Walt Disney World

At Walt Disney World, of course, the theme park is just one of many attractions—resort hotels, the Fort Wilderness camping area, championship golf courses, water recreation, and other vacation activities. All of this makes the Magic Kingdom's surroundings far different from those of its world-famous California predecessor.

Walt Disney World is the largest recreation enterprise ever undertaken by a single company. It is also a new kind of vacation experience...an all-in-one-place destination resort...a whole new "world" of recreation, relaxation, and entertainment. Some will choose to play here for a day at the Magic Kingdom, others to stay a week at the Polynesian Village or the Contemporary Resort Hotel or the Fort Wilderness campgrounds.

For Walt Disney World has already become "The Vacation Kingdom of the World"...or as LOOK magazine has said, "The Entertainment Spectacular of the Century!"

—The Story of Walt Disney World Commemorative Edition (1971)

Walt Disney World was never intended to be just another theme park or even the series of theme parks that it eventually became. The goal was to create a vacation destination where a guest would come for a multi-day stay.

To accomplish that goal, even from the original opening, there were other activities that ranged from renting water craft to horseback riding to golfing and many other options.

Today, Walt Disney World still offers those opportunities, along with two water parks, five championship golf courses, two mini-golf courses, fishing excursions, backstage tours, children's cruises, spas, a huge downtown shopping area, bicycle rentals, jogging on trails, bowling, water skiing, and the ESPN Wide World of Sports Complex, as well as special events throughout the year including the Epcot International Flower and Garden Festival and the Epcot International Food and Wine Festival.

The Walt Disney World Monorails

Zooming along on a sleek concrete beam high in the sky for nearly forty-five years, the brightly colored Walt Disney World monorails have provided eager park guests with not only a different perspective of the vacation destination, but also a glimpse of the transportation of the future.

According to Disney press information released in 1969 about the monorails at Walt Disney World:

> The principal means of travel from the parking center and main entrance to and from the theme park and hotels will be aboard the Walt Disney World-Alweg Monorail trains. Current plans call for the building of six five-car trains, some to stop at every hotel on the way around the circuit, while others carry passengers non-stop directly to the Magic Kingdom.

Those new monorails were dubbed the Mark IV and each one cost approximately $6 million to build.

They featured greater safety, comfort, and efficiency than the ones operating at Disneyland at the time. The Mark IV had a high capacity design that could hold up to 210 guests in the five-car train that was 171 feet long. There was improved air conditioning (considered vital in the Florida heat and humidity) and new door systems.

The Mark IV monorails were designed in Burbank under the direction of Imagineer Bob Gurr and built in Orlando by the Martin Marietta Corporation.

The seats in the Mark IV were a rich royal blue with four aisles of guests facing each other going across each car. Each car had four doors, except for the middle car that had a special double-door type of setup to allow for guests in wheelchairs.

Just like for the trams today, there were waiting queue slots for guests that held roughly the number of people who could fit in the empty seats in each aisle to help control the boarding. There was no standing room capability.

At the Magic Kingdom during the early days, guests boarded the monorail by going up the middle ramp and exited the train by going down the side ramps. It is the reverse today because it proved to cause congestion when the park closed at night and guests flooded out of the Magic Kingdom to leave.

In theory, it all sounded smooth and seamless. Yet on opening day in October 1971, only three monorails were operating. A fourth would be brought on later that month and a fifth was being constructed. Even with light attendance, it was not enough to handle all the guests clamoring to get to the park and spend their money.

Other forms of transportation were rushed into service, including six steam launches and other water craft like the Mike Fink keel boats from Frontierland. Half of the parking lot trams were needed to haul guests from the Ticket and Transportation Center to the Magic Kingdom, and they frequently overheated and broke down on the incline near the Contemporary Resort.

Today, the improved Mark VI version introduced by 1990 carries roughly 150,000 guests daily to their destinations at Walt Disney World, for a total of over 50 million guests per year.

Each Mark VI train consists of six cars. The overall length is 203 feet with a capacity of 365 passengers. The track consists of 26-inch wide, pre-cast concrete beams supported by concrete columns approximately 50 feet apart.

Each monorail travels on rubber tires and is powered by a 600-volt DC propulsion system which includes eight DC motors rated at 112 HP each, with the power emanating from each side of the beam.

Downtown Disney: In the Beginning

The Downtown Disney area used to be very different than what it is today with the recent expansion into Disney Springs that features fancy new eateries and merchandise shops.

In 1974, a few years after the opening of the Magic Kingdom, the Disney company built a collection of vacation villas, tree house villas, and a golf course that became the Disney Village Resort. The area would evolve into the Disney Institute and now the Saratoga Springs Resort and Spa.

Black Lake (which still borders the Preview Center building, and is now the home of the Amateur Athletic Union on Hotel Plaza Boulevard) was renamed Lake Buena Vista in 1969 with the incorporation of that town of the same name just up the street.

Walt Disney World actually has two small communities on property, Lake Buena Vista and Bay Lake, in order to meet the requirements necessary for it to be an improvement district (Reedy Creek Improvement District).

The canal system was widened into a large lake, called the Village Lagoon, next to the housing and golf course.

"Buena Vista" was chosen for its Disney connection: it was the name of the distribution company that released the Disney films, and also the name of the street in Burbank where the Disney Studio and corporate offices are located. Buena Vista is Spanish for "good view".

Right across the Village Lagoon from the Disney Village Resort was a small shopping area.

When it opened on March 22, 1975, the Lake Buena Vista Shopping Village was immediately popular with guests, locals, and business people as a location where they could purchase Disney merchandise and enjoy the Disney magic and quality service without having to pay to get into the Magic Kingdom or stay at one of the Disney resorts.

It had a quiet, soothing, small-town atmosphere where visitors could leisurely dine and shop and be entertained. It was a charming retail community surrounding the lake with a barber, post office, art gallery, pottery shop, candle shop, and pharmacy, as well as other simple businesses.

Eventually, it was renamed the Disney Village Marketplace and then it became the Downtown Disney Marketplace with the 1989 adjacent expansion into Pleasure Island, a location that mimicked downtown Orlando's popular Church Street, where themed restaurants and clubs operated.

The Pleasure Island area has been recently transformed into the new Disney Springs.

The original Lake Buena Vista Shopping Village had four places to eat: Lite Bite, Heidelberger's Deli, the Village Restaurant, and Cap'n Jack's (named after Disney Legend Jack Olsen, who had a fondness for sailing and fishing and was instrumental in the development of Disney theme park merchandise, beginning with Disneyland in 1955). All of these locations no longer exist.

Guests could also take a boat from Cruise Dock West to the Lake Buena Vista Club, where they could enjoy breakfast, lunch, and brunch, as well as French cooking at night.

The Downtown Disney area was meant to be a quiet, friendly oasis in the hectic and sometimes chaotic world of Disney. However, today it is as active and often as crowded as any of the theme parks.

Farewell to Cap'n Jack's

Cap'n Jack's Restaurant was an informal, New England-ish, nautically-themed restaurant at the Downtown Disney Marketplace on the east side. The restaurant had been a staple on the waterfront since the Lake Buena Vista Shopping Village opened in 1975.

Originally, it was called Cap'n Jack's Oyster Bar and was a location where adults could grab cocktails and appetizers in the early days of Walt Disney World. Obviously, it specialized in seafood, and was one of the very few locations on or near WDW property that was open until the wee hours.

The famous drink at the original Cap'n Jack's Oyster Bar was the strawberry margarita. It was the first East Coast appearance of this type of drink, which was quite popular with the cast members from California who had relocated to Florida, and spurred its introduction.

When the oyster bar became an official "restaurant" around 2000, the menu expanded and featured seafood, steak, pasta dishes, and kid-friendly items like chicken strips and hamburgers.

Not only was it the longest surviving original business in the Downtown area, it was the last remaining Disney-operated restaurant in that area as well. It was born along with now-forgotten locations such as the Gourmet Pantry, the Village Spirits, and so many others.

The entire area was not just a way to satisfy guests staying on Walt Disney property so that they didn't have to find transportation to downtown Orlando. It was meant to be a hub from which a housing community composed of town houses and condominiums would grow.

As part of the Phase Two plans for Walt Disney World, the monorail was to be extended to stop at the shopping and dining area, and some stanchion foundations were put in place and county clearances had been obtained.

Pricey shops selling elegant goods, from clothes to wine, were included to attract the local population as well as the tourists who could purchase items unavailable elsewhere in Orlando.

Cap'n Jack's unique hexagonal shape offered wonderful views of the lake and Downtown Disney's marina where guests could rent watercraft to leisurely cruise the nearby waterways.

Cap'n Jack's was built out into the lagoon and was described as a "floating" restaurant. The outside porch was intended for live female models to walk and display the newest in swimsuits from the nearby Windjammer Dock Shop (which had a red-headed mermaid as its logo).

The restaurant was named after Disney Legend Jack Olsen, who had a fondness for sailing and fishing. Olsen, who retired from the Disney company in 1977, was instrumental in shaping the Disney theme park merchandise mentality since the opening of Disneyland in 1955.

It was Olsen who jumped into dumpsters to rescue Disney animation cels, trim them into a cardboard matte, and then sell them for a dollar or so to early park guests. He was the one who insisted that Disney park merchandise be distinctly different than what guests could get anywhere else.

Like many of Disney's top executives, Olsen relocated from California to Florida to help open Walt Disney World, where he was the vice president in charge of Disney merchandise.

Cap'n Jack's last day of operation was August 17, 2013. Its closure was part of the conversion plan for the new Disney Springs, and it was located approximately where the new bridge is today.

However, the name lives on at the Cap'n Jack's Margarita Bar dockside and as the name of the marina.

The Birth of Walt Disney World Golfing

When Walt Disney World opened in October 1971, the company had to educate the general public that the new entertainment venue was not just like another Disneyland, but was an entire "vacation destination" featuring a wide variety of leisure activity.

Beautiful golf courses were always part of the original Florida Project plan, as conceived by Walt Disney himself. Walt had briefly taken up golfing as a hobby to alleviate stress.

In 1971, both the Magnolia and Palm golf courses, designed by Joseph L. Lee, opened. In 1993, Lee renovated the Magnolia.

Sandy Quinn, who was head of marketing for Disney World through its construction, opening, and the early years of its operation, said:

> You have to credit two people [with opening Walt Disney World on time]. Joe Fowler, the admiral, created all the levels of contractors and suppliers. He planned the invasion. Dick Nunis took them across the channel. They made a great team.

With a few weeks to go before the opening of Walt Disney World, Quinn was given the task of setting up a PGA golf tournament before the end of the year. Quinn knew nothing about arranging golf tournaments, but he did know that famed golfer Arnold Palmer was in town at his home in the new Bay Hill development. Quinn recalled:

> I sent somebody over to see if he would come by and at least talk to us about it. Well, he came over and we're starting to talk and all of a sudden he looks off in the distance, curious about something. I walk over and see he's watching the train engineers put the new cars on the monorail. Right away he gets interested and wants to know if he can take a ride.
>
> Well, as luck would have it, the engineers were running a full-scale test on the whole system that day—and they were delighted to have Arnie as their first passenger. But not nearly as delighted as Arnie. He jumped in one of the cars and that's where he stayed for about four hours. He was just like a kid, going 'round and 'round, waving and laughing, having a wonderful time.
>
> We said a small prayer, hoping the thing wouldn't fall down or something while he was in it. When he was through, we started talking

a little about a golf tournament. "No problem," he says, "sign me up. I'll call a few friends." And that was it. In no time at all, we had a full-fledged PGA golf tournament.

The Walt Disney World Open $150,000 Golf Championship was scheduled for November 29 through December 5, 1971. A $5,000 Pro-Am Tournament would take place on December 1, 1971. Jack Nicklaus won that year, and the following year, and the year after that.

Tiger Woods has won twice at Disney, including his rookie year on tour in 1996.

In 1973, the Walt Disney Open Invitational changed its name to the Walt Disney World Golf Classic. Golfing at Walt Disney World was so popular that the 125-room Golf Resort opened December 15, 1973, adjacent to the golf courses and near the Magic Kingdom.

In 1986, the Golf Resort became the Disney Inn, shifting the golf theme to a Snow White theme. It later became Shades of Green, an Armed Forces Recreation Center resort, when the U.S. Department of Defense leased the hotel from Disney in 1994 (and purchased it outright in 1996). It now has almost 600 rooms.

Typhoon Lagoon

Typhoon Lagoon opened on June 1, 1989, just across the street from the newly built Pleasure Island, with the world's largest outdoor surf pool (not just a wave pool).

Its creation was inspired by the success of the River Country water park located in Fort Wilderness Resort and Campground. The popularity of that attraction was so great that it could not accommodate all of the guests who wanted to enjoy it.

According to the back story created by the Disney Imagineers for the new water park:

> A furious storm once roared 'cross the sea, catching ships in its path, helpless to flee. Instead of a certain and watery doom, the winds swept them here, to Typhoon Lagoon.

That same fictitious storm from 1955, known as Hurricane Connie, also inflicted near total destruction on nearby Pleasure Island, owned by the descendants of Merriweather Adam Pleasure.

The typhoon drastically changed the small Placid Palms resort village, and to make matters worse, a subsequent earthquake and volcanic eruption left the community almost in complete ruins. Surfboards, fishing gear, boats, and other nautical items were flung wildly throughout the area. Trees toppled not only onto some of the buildings, but into them as well.

One old ship tanker was completely overturned, but today guests can walk into it and through the portholes see sharks and nearly 2,000 fish swimming by in a man-made reef. Many species of marine life, not necessarily native to the area, were deposited in the surrounding waters by the wind and water.

Even a pair of jaws from the fictional Sharkus Gigantus (reminiscent of an actual prehistoric shark known as a Megalodon) washed up on the beach.

The plucky inhabitants used their ill fortune to transform Placid Palms resort into the Leaning Palms resort, referencing the fact that some of the remaining palm trees were almost completely uprooted and now lean.

The local residents resourcefully rebuilt their town as best they could with the flotsam and jetsam of "found" objects. Imagineer Randy Bright summarized the effect back in the 1980s:

> Upon entering Typhoon Lagoon, guests find themselves in a ramshackle, tin-roofed island village landscaped with cargo, surfboards, and other marine wreckage left by the great storm.

Guests immediately see one of the unfortunate boats stuck atop the entrance sign as they turn off Buena Vista Boulevard to go toward Typhoon Lagoon. A series of signs inspired by the famous "Burma Shave" advertising roadside signs of yore, which told a story in rhyme on succeeding signs, tell the tale of Typhoon Lagoon in rhymed snippets before the guests even get to the parking lot.

The main entrance to Typhoon Lagoon is a mixture of bits and pieces of ships damaged during the typhoon. Wheelhouses and cabins were reformatted into ticket booths with a mast and a sail creating the marquee. High above the booths is a row of nautical flags that spell out "Welcome to Typhoon Lagoon".

On the right hand side is a sign that is a "key" to deciphering what letter of the alphabet each flag represents. Nearby is a line of flags that translate to "Piranha in pool".

Besides the non-stop water fun, guests can just stretch out and relax in the magnificently landscaped venue and enjoy some of the amusing storytelling details that surround them in this hidden oasis from the frantic theme park experience.

Blizzard Beach

After the opening of Typhoon Lagoon in 1989, the water park was so popular that it was filling to capacity on a daily basis and turning away hundreds of guests. Disney saw disappointed guests as well as potential profits going somewhere else.

Walt Disney Imagineering was given the task of developing a concept for another Walt Disney World water park. Several different ideas were proposed, but none of them matched the depth and whimsy of Typhoon Lagoon.

Imagineer Eric Jacobson's office was filled with a collection of little snow domes from his travels. One day, as he was distractedly playing with one of the globes, shaking it up so that the snow shapes swirled around the interior tableau, he mused: "Too bad we can't make a park out of one of these for guests to beat the Florida heat." While his peers considered it a joke, it was so strong a concept that they kept coming back to the idea.

According to Disney legend, Blizzard Beach was created by a meteorological phenomenon.

One balmy day, a freak winter storm developed over the western end of Walt Disney World and covered the area with a thick blanket of powdery white snow. Before you could say "hot cocoa", plans were underway for Florida's first ski resort.

Ski lifts were put up, toboggan runs were laid down, and an entire resort area blossomed around the mountain of snow. Yet before the first skier could strap on a pair of boots and stick his poles into the snow, the temperatures returned to their normal Florida levels and the powdery snow quickly turned into slippery slush. The ski resort operators saw their dream melting down the hillside.

The operators were preparing to cut their losses and walk away. However, they were interrupted by an echoing "YAHHOOO!!!" coming from the mountain of melting snow. They looked up to see a blue alligator, wearing a red scarf and gold inner tube, careening down the mountain at top speed. The raucous gator was a blue color because of the supposedly freezing temperatures and stayed that way even after things warmed up.

Ice Gator, who became the mascot of the area, landed in a pool of melted snow at the base of the mountain with a thunderous splash. The ski resort operators suddenly saw the park's potential, and the mountain of snow became Blizzard Beach, "the most slushy, slippery, exhilarating water park anywhere!"

Slalom courses and bobsled and toboggan runs became downhill waterslides. The creek of melted snow that formed at the base of the mountain became a relaxing tube ride. The chairlift carried swimmers instead of skiers. The ski jump on Mt. Gushmore became the tallest and fastest water slide in the world.

The park opened on April 1, 1995, and in 2014 hosted over two million guests, making it the third most visited water park in the world, right behind Typhoon Lagoon. It is larger than Typhoon Lagoon, with over seventeen slides, a wave pool, an area for pre-teens, and an area for children.

Hints of the Ice Gator abound, including the weather vane atop Lottawatta Lodge and his own little cottage along Cross Country Creek. Ice Gator was so popular that at one time he was a walk-around costumed character and was featured on numerous pieces of merchandise. He proved to be so successful that the Typhoon Lagoon water park created a cousin called Lagoona Gator who didn't capture the same affection from the guests.

Fantasia Gardens Mini-Golf

The Disney company's first miniature golf course, themed after the animated feature film *Fantasia* (1940), opened on May 20,1996, on eleven acres of land near the Walt Disney World Dolphin Resort. After the opening, Walt Disney Imaginering (WDI) Senior Concept Designer Joe Lanzisero said:

> Some of them [the items in the Fantasia Gardens' course] were no-brainers. Things people identify with when they think of *Fantasia*: elephants and hippos, snowflakes, mushrooms, Mickey and the brooms. We wanted soft, classical sequences that were more garden-like and fit the environment. That's why there's no "Rite of Spring" section (with its oversized dinosaurs).

The final plan included five sections from *Fantasia* that fit the gentle garden theme: "Toccata and Fugue", "the Nutcracker Suite", "the Pastoral Symphony", "Dance of the Hours", and finally, "the Sorcerer's Apprentice" as the dramatic conclusion.

For Fantasia Gardens, Joe Lanzisero was the senior concept designer along with another WDI concept designer, Robert Coltrin, who wrote the verses posted at each hole.

It was one of the first projects where WDI merged forces with DDC (Disney Development Company). DDC's Bob Kamerlander as construction manager and DDC's Paul Katen as project manager were assigned to the project. As Kamerlander stated

> I believe our relationship demonstrated the strengths of each organization: the creative talent that dreams up the Fantasia Gardens and the development expertise that transforms the concept into a terrific guest experience, as well as a financially viable asset for the company.

However, as with any large project, not everything went smoothly all the time. At one point, budget constraints threatened to eliminate the home of Zeus from the plans, but some creative re-working of the figures allowed Mount Olympus to be built. Lanzisero considered it to be the focal point that organized the rest of the design of the course.

On the 10th hole, where Bacchus is pouring wine down a hill, it is a more difficult shot than originally intended by the Imagineers.

Lanzisero said:

> After a misinterpretation of the design, the hill ended up being elevated about three feet higher than the drawings. But what it lacks in playability, it really makes up for in aesthetics.

Coltrin added:

> It is pretty steep, like a 45-degree angle. You putt up the hill and the ball comes down the other side like a pachinko game, going "bink, bink, bink, bink" as it hits the bubbles in the wine that he's pouring down the hill.

The goal was to orchestrate each hole with varying levels of difficulty. Some holes are fairly simple so that guests get an immediate payoff—for example, where the statue of a little faun plays a tune on his pipe when the ball drops into the hole. Coltrin enthused:

> Oh, the wonders of modern electronics! Digitize the music, put it into a microchip, and push it through a 50-watt amp, and two little, tiny speakers play it every time a ball drops in the cup. Nothing to it!

Some holes are more interactive than others. One of the favorites of the Imagineers is the 16th hole, with the statues of the brooms standing above the fairway. Lanzisero explained:

> Everyone gets the payoff here. You don't have to do anything special to get the brooms to dump the water. The water squirts not only over the putting area, but over where the people walk, too. This is programmed so that the buckets shoot water in sequence, but if you make it to the putting green in one shot, the ball has to go by three sensors so all the buckets splash at one time.

The Walt Disney World Casting Center

Architect Robert A.M. Stern designed the Walt Disney World Casting Center as an interpretation of the Doge's Palace in Venice, Italy.

He began work on the project in 1987 and the Casting Center opened in 1989.

Stern said:

> You have to remember that Disney is a dream world rooted in a dream view of life and of architectural history.

The Casting Center faces the busy I-4 freeway taking guests to the theme parks and acts as a whimsical castle-like billboard to attract employment applicants.

The building is approximately 61,000 square feet. The entrance is right across the street from Downtown Disney so that it would be easy to locate. Since Disney is a "show", its purpose is to cast for roles and not just hire employees for a job. That's why it's called a casting center.

The diamond patterns on the outside of the building hark back to the pattern found on the Italian harlequin, as well as being exaggerated references to the same triangular pattern on the exterior of the real Doge's Palace that was re-created at the Italy Pavilion in Epcot's World Showcase.

The canopy awning and turrets and crenellation (notches) seem to resemble the traditional Disney castles. That airplane-wing like canopy over the entrance was actually taken from concept drawings of Tomorrowland.

The Mickey Mouse head-shaped cut-outs along the top of the building serve a practical purpose. They are scuppers, so when it rains, the water on the roof drains through them.

The bronze doorknobs are re-creations of the famous doorknob in Disney's animated feature *Alice in Wonderland*. The smiling doorknob is truly a Disney character, since he does not exist in Lewis Carroll's original story.

After entering the building, a short walk leads to a small oval rotunda surrounded by 12 gold leaf-covered statues of Disney characters on pillars, just as you might find sculptures on pillars in an Italian palace.

At this point, the only way you can turn is to the left, to ascend a ramp 150 feet long.

As you walk up the ramp, there are paintings on either side that once again mimic the murals that would be found in an Italian villa. However, the paintings on the side of the building facing the real world and paralleling I-4 depict unhappiness and road hazards. Even Mickey Mouse is getting a traffic ticket from a police officer.

The paintings on the side of the building facing Walt Disney World property and your potential future depict the Disney characters enjoying themselves tremendously at the parks, and even a smiling Walt Disney looking out on his dream that he never lived to see finished.

In addition to these murals, there are cracks on the wall and under the bridge. During the Renaissance, newly wealthy Italian families wanted to make their estates look old and ancestral, and so used the effect of trompe l'oeil (fooling the eye) of painting cracks to create the illusion of antiquity.

From a distance these cracks look amazingly real, but they are flush with the wall. This imperfection is also designed to make the applicant feel more comfortable that not every thing is perfect.

The vaulted ceiling and natural lighting also provide relaxation through a sense of "openness". And looking up, applicants can see Peter Pan flying toward Neverland, or in this case, a central receiving desk to guide them to the proper location.

The Walt Disney World Casting Center is just another example of clever Disney storytelling through architecture.

Two Forgotten WDW Christmas Traditions

At one time, Walt Disney World had several holiday traditions that were unique to the theme park, including the Jolly Holidays Dinner Show and the Glory and the Pageantry of Christmas show.

Despite their huge popularity with park guests, they disappeared before the turn of the current century and were not replaced with any other option.

Those Jolly, Jolly, Jolly Holidays! Those Holly, Holly, Holly Jolly Days! All the decorations! Many celebrations! Many happy faces! Cozy fireplaces! Let the bells ring out now! Everyone sing out now!

The Jolly Holidays Dinner Show at Disney's Contemporary Resort was performed from 1992 through the 1998 Christmas season, when it was discontinued. The Fantasia Ballroom was converted into an immersive theater-in-the-round setting with more than a hundred talented performers in a musical extravaganza. Besides the raised main stage, there were several smaller stages on the outer perimeter of the tables.

Performers spilled out into the audience, as well. The show took place at Holiday Village where the patriarch of the town, known simply as Papa (and looking a bit like a grey-bearded Sebastian Cabot with a deep, gravelly voice), recalled his memories of the holidays.

Mickey, Minnie, Pluto, Goofy, and Chip'n'Dale cavorted with perky singers and dancers. The Country Bears dropped by to play a tune before they went back out into the snow to play. There was even a short version of the "Nutcracker Suite" featuring the hippos and ostriches from *Fantasia*. Of course, some scenes seemed to be borrowed from other shows, including the tap dancing horses for the sleigh ride, the marching toy soldiers, and Santa Goofy making an appearance.

In addition, guests enjoyed an all-you-can-eat feast of fresh-cooked turkey, honey-baked ham, and other holiday treats. It was a hugely popular show, often completely sold out even at a premium price, although significant changes were made in its final year that did not please everyone.

For more than fifteen years during the 1980s and 1990s, the Disney Village Marketplace (now known as Downtown Disney) ushered in the season with a performance of the Glory and the Pageantry of Christmas. It was a traditional "living nativity scene" re-enactment that was originally performed at the open-air pavilion known as the Captain's Tower (now Pin Traders), but soon moved to the larger venue of the Waterfront Dock Stage. The shopping area nearby was decorated to suggest a re-creation of the little town of Bethlehem.

It was such a popular and dignified show that guests did not mind standing in line for hours for a chance to see it. "The Christmas Story", narrated by Kevin Miles (whose deep baritone voice could also be heard in venues like Epcot's Voices of Liberty and Magic Kingdom's Dapper Dans) and interspersed with Christmas songs, was amazingly simple.

Mary and Joseph approach the manger and she reveals a child wrapped in swaddling clothes. The shepherds come in. The angels appear, rising up from behind the manger. There was a total cast of 36 performers.

The narration told how the shopkeepers of the village brought gifts, including cheese from the dairyman and breads from the baker. Sadly, one little orphan child had no gift to bring. To the strains of the song "Little Drummer Boy", a small child walks up to the manger and, encouraged by Mary, plays his drum.

There was no official announcement of the reason for the show's cancellation, but there were rumors that it had grown so popular that large audiences caused logistical challenges. There were also grumblings that the show was not substantially increasing sales at the nearby shops.

The Empress Lilly Story

The Lake Buena Vista Shopping Village became the Walt Disney World Village at Lake Buena Vista in 1977.

Heralding that change was the introduction of the Empress Lilly that officially opened on May 1, 1977. This steam ship was named after Walt Disney's widow, Lillian Bounds Disney, who was there on opening day to christen her namesake.

However, the Empress Lilly was not a boat even though her paddle-wheel churned constantly in the early days, as if she were ready to steam out of port, but rather a building built to resemble a boat anchored on a submerged concrete foundation. At 220 feet long by 62 feet wide, she was over twice the size of the Magic Kingdom steamboats.

The Lilly became home to the first Walt Disney World character breakfasts.

The upscale Empress Lounge featured a live harpist, a tradition carried on at Victoria & Albert's in the Grand Floridian Resort. The Empress Room was elegantly decorated in the style of Louis XV and men were required to wear ties and jackets to dine there, just as they are today at Victoria & Albert's.

A more raucous time was to be had at the full bar in the Baton Rouge Lounge, with comedy and Dixieland jazz by the Riverboat Rascals show band. The room's décor was primarily red, a visual play on the lounge's name, with the same red carpet that covered the floor of the special Lillian VIP car on the Disneyland Railroad. Lillian loved the color and used it to decorate the Disney's private apartment above the firehouse in Disneyland.

Above the Baton Rouge was the Fisherman's Deck restaurant specializing in fresh fish caught daily. For those who preferred meat, there was the Steerman's Quarters steakhouse restaurant with its well-remembered Angus beef offerings (as well as lamb and veal) served to guests who could look out the window at the giant churning paddlewheel.

On the third floor was the Captain's Table. Inside this private banquet hall was a 24-foot long parquet table, imported from New Orleans Square at Disneyland, which seated up to 20 guests.

During an interview in 1982, Dick Nunis revealed that the area near the Empress Lilly was to be expanded into a New Orleans section similar in style to Disneyland's New Orleans Square. The buildings would house shops on the lower level and hotel rooms on the upper levels. Apparently, the storyline was now that the Empress Lilly had just pulled in to the dock to unload goods and passengers at Port Orleans.

But this was a time of turmoil for the Disney company, and so that expansion was never realized, although later a Port Orleans resort was built not far away.

With the opening of Pleasure Island, the story behind the Empress Lilly changed once again. Now, it was the original home of the fabled Merriweather Adam Pleasure and his family, and it had brought them to the island where Pleasure built his empire and permanent residence.

On April 22, 1995, the Empress Lilly closed her doors, and had the interior gutted in preparation for a new dining experience and a new owner, the Levy Restaurants, who had signed a 20-year license to operate at the location. The smokestacks, signage, and paddlewheel were removed from the exterior, and on March 10, 1996, it reopened as Fulton's Crab House, with new giant gaudy red neon signs to theme in to the rest of the Pleasure Island buildings.

PART FOUR

The Rest of the Story

The first purchases of central Florida land by Disney under the name of several bogus real estate companies was recorded on May 3, 1965, and included one for 8,380 acres of swamp and brush from State Senator Irlo Bronson. The deal had been made seven months earlier.

The first newspaper account of the large-scale interest in Orange and Osceola county property ran the next day. A story in the May 4th *Orlando Sentinel* reported that the transactions "will undoubtedly increase rumors already afloat for the past year to the effect that a new and large industrial complex is about to locate in this area".

It was speculated that a car manufacturing company like Ford, or a space or aircraft project like NASA's Manned Orbiting Laboratory Project, or millionaires like the Rockefellers or Howard Hughes were secretly purchasing the land. One account even suggested the Mafia was buying land to launder ill-gotten gains or dump bodies in the swamps.

However, no credence was put in the rumor of an East Coast Disneyland, because Walt Disney himself had specifically denied it when interviewed during a recent visit to Cape Kennedy. He told the reporter that he was investing so much to expand Disneyland during its tencennial year that he did not have the interest or finances for any other venture.

Within three weeks of recording the Bronson transaction, Florida Ranch Lands had wrapped up deals with 47 owners. Eventually, the firm negotiated agreements with 51 owners to buy some 27,400 acres for more than $5 million at an average price of $182 per acre.

In October 1965, Emily Bavar, editor of the *Orlando Sentinel's* Sunday supplement magazine, attended a press junket to Disneyland for its tenth anniversary and had the opportunity to corner Walt Disney himself.

Walt's evasiveness and his in-depth knowledge of central Florida when she quizzed him about being behind the land purchases there encouraged her to write a story on October 21, 1965, that the mystery buyer was Disney. After further investigation, the *Sentinel* headlined its Sunday edition three days later with "We Say 'Mystery Industry' is Disney".

Florida Governor Burns confirmed the story on October 25 and the formal announcement took place in Orlando on November 15, 1965.

Fred Joerger

Some guests miss the breathtaking atrium waterfall featured in the lobby of the Polynesian Village Resort that was removed in 2014. That was the work of Imagineer Fred Joerger.

In his 1982 guide to Walt Disney World, travel writer Steve Birnbaum stated, in reference to River Country at Fort Wilderness:

> Fred Joerger—the same Disney rock builder who created Big Thunder Mountain, Schweitzer Falls at the Jungle Cruise, and the caves of Tom Sawyer Island (among other things) at the Magic Kingdom—has helped design scores of rocks used to landscape one of the largest swimming pools in the state. More have been piled into a small mountain for guests to climb up—and then slide down. The rocks, scattered with pebbles acquired from stream beds in Georgia and the Carolinas, look so real that it's hard to believe they aren't.

Imagineer Fred Joerger joined the Disney company in 1953, and his job was to make three-dimensional models of the drawings that artists did, including the model of Disneyland's Sleeping Beauty Castle and the one of the *Mark Twain* steamboat. Walt preferred having a three-dimensional model to consult rather than just a drawing on paper.

Walt Disney found Joerger's contribution to the Pirates of the Caribbean attraction so crucial that he had Joerger flown from the Disney Studio in Burbank to Disneyland in Orange County every day for nine months because Walt didn't want him stressed by freeway traffic.

In 1997, I asked Joerger how he became Walt Disney World's resident rock expert, and he burst out with a huge laugh. He said:

> It happened quite by accident. Opening my big mouth at the wrong time. Because I had built the models for all of the rock work down there [in Orlando], and when they had just gotten started on the construction of the Magic Kingdom, I went down there for one weekend,

really to just check out what was going on. I walked into the Jungle Cruise where Marc [Davis] had designed this keen waterfall, the one where the elephants were bathing.

Well, gosh, nothing resembled the models. They hadn't even looked at the models. I don't think they had even looked at the drawings, because where the elephant is supposed to be sitting taking a shower, he couldn't possibly have gotten wet if he had tried.

I made a series of phone calls. I didn't know one end of a plaster trowel from another. These fellas who were building the thing said, "What do you want us to do?" I said, "Well, just go ahead doing what you're doing (because there was a tight deadline to opening day), only let me come down and give you a little help and we'll do it a little differently." And, so, that was my introduction to it. I guess they thought I was good at it because from there on I got stuck with it all the time. Rocks, rocks, and more rocks.

For both Disneyland and Walt Disney World, Joerger did the intricately detailed rockwork for Big Thunder Mountatin Railroad. He retired from Imagineering in 1979, but returned as a field art director for the opening of Epcot (concentrating on the Canadian Rockies in the Canada Pavilion) and to supervise the rock work in Tokyo Disneyland. He was made a Disney Legend in 2001, and died in 2005 at the age of 91.

His faux headstone outside The Haunted Mansion reads: "Here lies Good Old Fred, a great big rock fell on his head."

Michael Graves

Former Disney CEO Michael Eisner once claimed that the two lega-
cies he would leave for Disney theme parks were improved culinary
offerings and entertainment architecture.

By the time Michael Eisner became chairman and CEO of the
Disney company in 1984, the company's connection to innovative
themed resorts had faded, although the number of guests coming
to Disney World had greatly increased.

Eisner rejected a plan to build two rather ordinary hotel towers
(that he referred to as "refrigerator boxes") near Epcot.

After some legal wrangling with the Tishman Corporation, Eisner
hired award-winning Princeton architect Michael Graves—who had
never designed a hotel before—to design the Walt Disney Swan and
Dolphin hotels.

The hotels were necessary to accommodate the convention groups
who were staying at off-property hotels that had greater convention
space than the existing Disney resorts. When the two hotels opened
in 1989 and 1990, they offered the largest hotel convention space in
the southeastern United States.

Over the years, the design of the hotels has been the source of
much discussion (not all of it flattering). It was planned that way,
to bring attention to the concept of entertainment architecture by
leading architects.

The Dolphin is to represent a tropical island that has been thrust
violently out of the sea, which accounts for the dolphins on top and
the banana leaves along the side. This act created massive waves that
splashed up on the nearby hotel where two swans were turned into
stone as they observed this catastrophic event.

Graves deliberately selected two creatures that "were not part of
the existing Disney mythology", but had hopes that they would then
be developed further as Disney icons once he had selected them.

He based his dolphins on the work of Italian sculptor Bernini, but their mouths curved downward, and Eisner insisted that wasn't going to happen on Walt Disney World property—so Graves' dolphins have their mouths curved upwards, as if smiling.

Graves said:

> Both inside and out, the hotel was designed to echo the tropical Florida landscape, as well as the fun and whimsy of the nearby Disney attractions and an aura of fantasy that appeals to guests of all ages.

In March 1997, Graves was working on the post office for the city of Celebration that he described as the "smallest building in the city" and was amused that he was responsible for the smallest building and the largest building (Disney's Dolphin hotel) currently on Disney World property.

For his first architectural assignment for the Disney company, Graves had designed the Team Disney corporate building in Burbank, California.

During a meeting with Michael Eisner, Graves said that Eisner told him:

> Look, everyone here will have some design priorities for you, but I only have one priority. When I come in to work each morning and go up to my office, I'll probably have very little to smile about. So do something that will make me smile when I arrive.

When his first designs for the Team Disney building were rejected, Graves came up with the concept of having the Seven Dwarves as caryatids. A caryatid is a sculpted figure serving as an architectural support taking the place of a column or a pillar supporting horizontal bands. Graves explained:

> Because *Snow White and the Seven Dwarfs* was truly the foundation of the Disney Studio and supported the growth of the company, just as the dwarfs are supporting the building.

William Robertson

William Robertson was a Disney character sculptor who worked with Disney Legend and master sculptor Blaine Gibson before becoming self-employed. WDW hired him to build frames for topiaries, which he did in the backyard of his College Park home. One of those topiaries is the fourteen-foot-long bison in front of the entrance to the Wilderness Lodge that opened in 1994.

Robertson was also responsible for the topiaries in the Johnny Depp film *Edward Scissorhands* (1990).

Bundled in these supportive logs of the Wilderness Lodge lobby are many carvings by Robertson showing the four levels of animal life existing in the wilderness.

On the lowest level you find the creatures of the field and meadows, such as the turkey, raccoon, squirrel, and rabbit. The animals on the next level are those of the lower mountains, such as the wolf, pronghorn antelope, bison, and elk. On the third are those of the high mountain, such as the mountain goat, sheep, bear, and mountain lion. The highest level has the birds of prey, including the falcon, American bald eagle, hawk. and owl.

It took four tons of wood to create these creatures. On average, it was ten days to carve each animal using an electric saw, rotary saw, a chisel, and a hammer.

Robertson did massive research and then rendered drawings that he used to create scale clay or plaster models as guides.

Mountain goats and some Rocky Mountain sheep look similar, so Robertson had to emphasize the subtle differences in head shapes.

Disney suggested animals for Robertson, but the artist said that after that point he had a free hand:

> 'I had to know how to fit the animals into the trees. Each animal had to be carved around the limbs, knots and rotten spots. There was no way to change the tree.

Robertson said that he wanted to "show the mark of the hands of the artist—not slick, but a rough, human feeling". He continued:

> Disney will try and do something artificially to meet fire codes or to get it to be weather-resistant. But in this instance everything was done in the traditional way, by the artist, by hand.

Every night during the six months before the hotel's Memorial Day opening, Robertson climbed scaffolds to chisel into the pine trees. "We finished the day before the hotel opened," he laughed.

Robertson's sculpture work can be seen on the six brass animals at the check-in desk that were purposely positioned at a children's level so they could be petted by curious youngsters. The beavers in the elevator holding a long stick that is used as a railing are also Robertson's creation.

As a bit of whimsy, Robertson took months to carve the cedar character totem pole outside the gift shop that features Mickey Mouse, Goofy, Donald Duck, and Humphrey the Bear (the official mascot of the resort). Robertson said:

> This wasn't necessarily just another traditional Disney image. That was rather exciting as an artist. I had freedom to have a little fun. I called an artist in Oregon to get advice on how to handle that kind of wood. I'd never have chosen cedar. It has to be kept sopping wet to cut it. But the other totem poles were done in cedar.
>
> The only problem was there was a lot of work to be done within a short period of time.

Marvin Davis

Marvin Aubrey Davis was born in Clovis, New Mexico, on December 21, 1910. He attended both UCLA and USC in Los Angeles, Californis, where he graduated with a degree in architecture in 1935, and received the American Institute of Architects medal as the top student of his class.

Two years later, he was working at 20th Century Fox as an art director on such films as *Gentlemen Prefer Blondes* and *The Asphalt Jungle*. In 1953, he became part of WED (Walt Disney Imagineering).

It was Davis who went through over a hundred different designs to come up with the diagrammatic plan for Disneyland with its distinctive shape and central hub.

In 1955, Davis married Walt Disney's favorite niece, Marjorie Sewell. He remembered:

> At one point, I actually went up to his office and I said, "Walt, I'm going to marry Margie." He just said, "Go ahead." When Walt heard that Margie was going to marry me, he said to her, "You know, he's a very stubborn man." Maybe Walt liked that in me because he was a hell of a lot more stubborn than I am.

Marjorie was one of the first live-action Disney stars appearing in the educational film *Clara Cleans Her Teeth* in 1926.

When Walt was visiting Florida anonymously to check out the property, he borrowed the Davis last name. On these visits, Walt used the pseudonym "Walter E. Davis" so that the initials "WED" matched the initials on Walt's luggage and other items.

After years being an art director on Disney live-action films, in 1965 Marvin Davis returned to WED as a project designer for Walt Disney World. He devised the master plan for the Magic Kingdom theme park, and also contributed to the design of the Contemporary, the Polynesian, and the Golf Resort.

As Imagineer Marty Sklar recalled:

A source of great pride for him, though, was that when he came back to Imagineering to do Walt Disney World, it took him only seven versions. That's remarkable considering that Walt Disney World was 27,000 acres, a big puzzle that he had to sort out and make understandable for guests. A lot of people worked on that plan, but it was Marvin who brought it all together.

Walt Disney World landscaper Bill Evans remembered:

> The remarkable thing about Marvin was his attitude. He could have been angry about his ailment [Marvin suffered from the effects of polio], but he was always up, always positive, always in good spirits. He never let it affect him. He was cheerful, creative, and an inspiration to everyone who knew him.
>
> One time, in the summer of 1967, we were trying to get a better look at the site in Florida. It was hotter than Hades that day, 100 degrees and humidity in the 90s. We crammed into Land Rovers and ours got stuck in the mud. There was no one around the 28,000 acres at that time except for an occasional hunter chasing a deer, so I had to leave Marvin behind while I slogged through the mud looking for the others. When we finally got back to him, he wasn't as cheerful as usual, but I guess you wouldn't be either if you had to sit in that heat and humidity for several hours.

Davis officially retired in 1975 and died on March 8, 1998, in Santa Monica, California, at the age of 87. He was made a Disney Legend in 1994.

Peter Dominick Jr.

During the era of former Disney CEO Michael Eisner, noted architects were recruited to expand the vision of Walt Disney World and were given prominent recognition in all the publicity and an extraordinary amount of artistic freedom.

In August 1992, at the ground-breaking ceremony for Disney's Wilderness Lodge, Eisner said:

> In our architecture, Disney continues to produce the kind of ground-breaking entertainment that keeps the Disney name magical to people around the world. Our architecture is part of the show.

Peter Dominick Jr., who headed the Urban Design Group of Denver, Colorado, and was an avid outdoorsman, had been commissioned to design the upscale Wilderness Lodge near the Magic Kingdom.

Dominick was well known for having a great passion and understanding of the building traditions of the Rocky Mountain West.

As part of the research for the new Disney resort, Dominick and members of the Disney Development Company visited lodges at Yosemite, Yellowstone, and Glacier national parks.

Dominick recalled that when he presented his initial design to Eisner that:

> Michael Eisner leapt up from the conference table to examine the drawing more closely, challenging his creative team to accept our idea.

> During these halcyon years of Disney, when Eisner was being hailed as a modern-day Medici, we worked with one of the great creative companies of its time and collaborated with the most talented designers, working at their most creative boundaries.

Dominick's primary inspirations for the Wilderness Lodge were the Old Faithful Inn at Yellowstone Natural Park and the Awahwanee Lodge in Yosemite National Park that are referenced in his final design.

He recalled:

> [Disney's Wilderness Lodge] does, in fact, capture the spirit and sense of place one associates with our national parks, icons of our American heritage...with their art, architecture, and dramatic landscapes.
>
> There are romantic and endearing qualities associated with the early national parks movement—the Northwest, the Native Americans, the great lodges. All of these elements have been combined in wonderful detail, creating a unique wilderness experience.

Dominick was inspired by Stephen Mather, the first director of the National Park Service, who insisted on using whatever building materials were indigenous to an area in building a hotel so that it blends all aspects together and becomes more organic to the area.

This style was known as "rustic architecture". The concept was that art, architecture, and landscape should be fully integrated in the design and construction of the building.

Dominick set out to create a log hotel from the early 1900s in the Northwest Rockies incorporating authentic Native American elements, natural lightning, and wherever possible, actual building material like natural limestone.

Eighty-five loads of lodge pole pines were harvested from "standing dead forests" (where the tree had been killed from some natural cause like insects or volcano soot) in Oregon and Montana to build the resort. No living trees were chopped down to create the lodge poles. Stretched end to end, they would be forty miles long.

The wood floor in the lobby is composed of Brazilian cherry, White Oak, Bird's Eye Maple, and Burl Walnut.

Only the rockwork is fabricated, using gunite. Real rocks were used to create molds for cement that was later spray painted to look like granite or sandstone.

So don't take it for "granite".

Dominick's work on the Wilderness Lodge was so well-received by guests and critics that he went on to design the Animal Kingdom Lodge at Disney World and the Grand Californian resort in Anaheim for the Disney company. Dominick passed away at the age of 67 in 2009.

The First WDW Resorts

In 1967, the Disney company created a full-color map to indicate the various resort hotels that would surround the Magic Kingdom theme park. The company wanted them to capture the same Disney magic and storytelling that was evident in the attractions.

That map showed a Cape Cod Village, a South Seas glass skyscraper in the shape of a pyramid, Yesterday Hotel (to theme in with Main Street, U.S.A.; at one point, it was going to be located inside the park itself, in the building that now houses the Town Square Theater), Frontier Village, Spanish Colonial Hotel, Oriental Motel, the Dutch Hotel, and the African Hotel (to theme in with Adventureland).

In addition, there were locations in the front of the Magic Kingdom earmarked for an ice rink and a roller dome.

By 1969, these possible resorts had been narrowed down to Disney Persian Palace, U.S.A. Disney (that would become briefly Tempo Bay Resort and finally the Contemporary Resort), Far East Disney, Venice Disney, and Disney South Pacific. Frontier Village was renamed Diamond D (for Disney) Dude Ranch on its way to becoming Fort Wilderness Resort and Campgrounds.

Of course, these were not the final names, but placeholders to give a sense of the type of resort that would be built. For example, the Contemporary was indeed originally called "the Contemporary", but that was not intended to be its name, just a description of what the theme of the place should reflect.

When Imagineer John Hench and others pitched the name Tempo Bay for the resort, Walt's older brother Roy, who was leading the company, looked at them and said, "What's wrong with the name 'contemporary'? I like it."

So the hotel retained that name.

Financial challenges, including the 1973 gas crisis, prevented the building of additional resorts for over a decade.

When the Disney company determined they would run the WDW resort hotels themselves, John Curry was put in charge. Curry was personally hired by Walt Disney in August 1966 to oversee the hotel division and is usually considered the first person hired to work at Walt Disney World.

Born in Yosemite National Park at Camp Baldy, which was one of a number of park properties his parents operated, Curry grew up helping run the operations after his father died at an early age. The family's company was Amfac, the successor to the Fred Harvey Company.

Walt met Curry in the 1960s at Yosemite, where Walt was scouting opportunities to build a Mineral King hotel and ski park.

Working with architects, Curry and his team laid groundwork for five Walt Disney World hotels, including three that were never built: the Asian, the Venetian, and the Persian. Curry left Orlando in 1972 for Hilton Head, South Carolina, and soon became president of his own condominium development consulting firm.

Originally, the Florida theme park would have looked much different than what finally appeared. In fact, Imagineer Claude Coats created concept art for an attraction that would have been placed between the Contemporary Resort and the back of Tomorrowland, and use the water of nearby Bay Lake.

According to Imagineer Tony Baxter, Coats always loved dinosaurs and helped design the ones for the 1964 New York World's Fair. Guests would have been able to board a twisting water ride to journey into the prehistoric past to confront life-sized dinosaurs.

The Three Missing Magic Kingdom Resorts

In 1970, the Disney company announced:

> The hotels are called "theme resorts" because everything from interior décor to employees' costumes and dining room menus will carry out an overall theme. Two hotels, the Contemporary- and the Polynesian, will open the first year. The Asian, Persian, and Venetian will follow later in the Phase One plan.

The Phase One plan for Walt Disney World was that not everything could be built and operational by October 1971, but would be added within the first five years.

> The Asian hotel will be strongly Thai in its motif. A theme restaurant and lounge at the top of its 160-foot tower building will provide an enchanting setting for nighttime dancing and stage show entertainment. Each of its 600 rooms, including 50 elegant suites in royal Thai décor, will look out on the lagoon or a central recreation area.

The Asian resort hotel was scheduled to open by 1973. Land had been cleared and prepared where the Disney's Grand Floridian Resort and Spa stands today. A square plot of land prominently jutted out into the Seven Seas Lagoon and the nearby road had been dubbed Asian Way. There were also plans to have large meeting rooms under the guest area of the resort for conventions.

The Asian had gotten to the point that an approved sample interior for the rooms was completed, and elaborate Oriental gardens had been designed by landscaper Bill Evans. Guest rooms would have been arranged in a square around the perimeter, with two-thirds of the rooms having beautiful garden or lake views. The remainder of the rooms would have been in the tower building providing a view into the central recreation area that would probably have featured a themed pool.

At the Venetian resort, an enclosed small boat harbor and intricate system of waterways will recreate the Old World charm of the famed Italian "City of Canals". Shopping will be a unique experience as guests travel by gondola along "streets of water" and under ornate bridges linking various sections of the resort. The style is reminiscent of St. Mark's Square, complete with a 120-foot campanile which will toll the time. The entire lobby will be glass-topped, creating a brilliant, sunlit atrium effect indoors.

Located between the Contemporary Resort and the Ticket and Transportation Center near the water bridge on the Seven Seas Lagoon, the Venetian would have resembled the current Italy Pavilion in Epcot's World Showcase.

Stepping right out of the Arabian Nights is the Persian resort which will reign like an exotic far-Eastern palace on the Northwest shore of the lake. Jewel-like mosques and columns will rise above landscaped courtyards, while terraced sundecks offer sculpted swimming pools and "old Persian" dining facilities. Guest will practically be able to sail to their own rooms through a sheltered marina.

Located to the north and slightly east of the Contemporary Resort on Bay Lake, the Persian would have been laid out in a circular pattern with a large central building featuring a twenty-four-foot blue dome. Smaller blue domes would have highlighted the white columns and buildings.

After a stop at the Contemporary, the monorail would have journeyed to the Persian. From there, instead of going directly to the Ticket and Transportation Center, the monorail would take a short detour through nearby Tomorrowland, just like the monorail at Disneyland.

These unbuilt resorts were meant to create an exotic and unique experience for Disney World guests from the seven seas of the world. That's why it is the Seven Seas Lagoon.

World Showcase Pavilions

In 1978, several country pavilions were announced for the World Showcase including Russia (with a re-creation of Red Square), Denmark, Iran (when the Shah of Iran was in power), and Switzerland (with a Matterhorn and the bobsled attraction), as well as the following:

Israel On the shorelines of the Israel Pavilion, the ruins of an ancient minaret serves as an information center. Olive and cypress trees line the entrance and provide shade for buildings and traveler alike. Beyond the pavilion's entrance, the rising walkways lead travelers to a courtyard with shops clustered around the perimeter. The bazaar atmosphere of a marketplace in Israel permeates the interior and exterior of the shops. Tapestries, custom wood and brass items, jewelry, fashion apparel, and quality gifts provide guests with a small piece of Israel to take home.

United Arab Emirates Guests will immediately pass two ancient Arabic dhows (sailing ships). Inside the pavilion, visitors first experience the excitement of a re-created Bedouin encampment. Located at the center of this deserted oasis will be the traditional ascetic black tents that symbolize Arabian warmth and hospitality. Then, guests are beckoned by the opulent royal marquis to enter an Arabian Nights experience, a thrilling magic-carpet ride through the Arab world's most fascinating cultures, both past and present. As guests glide above the courtyard area, a powerful mythical character appears before them to serve as narrator and guide through the adventure.

Spain Take a spectacular journey through Spain by film to little-known and out-of-the-way vacation Edens. A ride attraction captures the country's passionate heritage and spirit in her arts. In a waterside restaurant indulge in tapas, or Spanish-style finger food—a blend of varied ingredients, but suitable to simple tastes. And browse the marketplaces of striking contrast, from pueblo village to aristocratic opulence.

Costa Rica The architecture would have been Spanish colonial with a crystal palace containing a sample of the tropical gardens of Costa Rica with an orchid show at the entrance. The conservatory would cover nearly a third of an acre with beautiful flora, waterfalls, and tropical birds to create a relaxing atmosphere. Outside would be a snack bar serving seafood and melons. Leather items, carved wood, and similar items would be sold in the craft and merchandise area

One of the most interesting things about the Costa Rica Pavilion was that the incredibly detailed model mysteriously disappeared soon after the presentation to the government officials, prompting an extensive investigation, but the model was never recovered. Imagineer David Mumford claimed:

> The model was one of the best we've ever built. It was insured so we recovered the money, but I think we lost a real treasure.

Equatorial Africa A pavilion was designed to be located on the land between China and Germany. The centerpiece icon was a huge treehouse similar to ones that African tribesmen might have built and would have housed an immersive film experience of wild animals gathering at a waterhole at dusk.

The pavilion would have included a film presentation on the history of Africa written and hosted by Alex Haley, the Pultizer Prize-winning author of the novel *Roots*, and entitled *Africa Rediscovered*. There would also have been a "Sound Safari" where guests walked a lushly landscaped pathway and heard the animals behind the foliage. The finale of that experience would have been a walk through a dark cave during a feeding frenzy with lions.

In addition, the pavilion would have featured African musicians and dancers as well as a small museum with rotating exhibits of African art.

Wilderness Junction

In 1976, Edward Prizer, editor of *Orlando-Land* magazine, had lunch with Dick Nunis, who at the time was executive vice president of both Disneyland and Walt Disney World.

At that moment in time, Nunis was preparing after the short interview to put on a pair of boots and stake out a bunch of new campsites at Fort Wilderness Resort and Campgrounds. He spoke to Prizer about the upcoming Epcot project:

> What Walt really wanted was to show the world how private industry can take virgin land and develop it properly through the free enterprise system.
>
> We have to continue to add to the theme park. We had a walk-through today. We were talking about a whole new expansion. I spend a day a month walking through with the creative staff. The theme park is designed to go north.

Nunis mentioned that one of the reasons River Country was a favorite of his was that Walt Disney himself came up with the idea long ago, based on an old swimming hole where he went as a kid. He planned to put it in Disneyland, but there wasn't room and the idea gathered dust until they brought it out for Walt Disney World.

Nunis said there were plans to add a stockade and a replica of a frontier town to the Fort Wilderness Resort and campground:

> We're going to have lots of fun things there. I've always wanted to do a fun place called Sadie Mae's Palace. Another thing we'll have in the old town will be Granny Kincaid's Farm where kids can pet animals and jump in the hay. That's another of Walt's ideas that we never developed.
>
> Fort Wilderness has room for 350–400 more campsites. Then we'll go somewhere else and build another campground. More bike paths are going to be added. We have a mile of trails around the campground. We'll add more to connect with the Contemporary, the Polynesian,

and the Magic Kingdom. We'll be building paths for five years and we will have ten miles of them.

In 1992, the Disney company announced a new addition to the Fort Wilderness area that was strongly supported by Nunis and called at the time Buffalo Junction (later referred to as Wilderness Junction).

The plans were to build an upscale 600-room resort between Disney's Fort Wilderness Resort and Campground and the Wilderness Lodge. It would have been themed to the Old West of Dodge City. One of the main attractions would have been a version of Disneyland Paris' Buffalo Bill Wild West Show, prompting the name Buffalo Junction originally.

The bottom level of the buildings would have shops and restaurants, while the upper levels would have rooms for guests. All three resorts would have been connected with a new operating version of the Fort Wilderness Railroad.

The story would begin at Fort Wilderness, representing the original frontier period of the United States. Wilderness Junction would showcase the expansion out to the Wild West, and, finally, the story would end at Wilderness Lodge, where Americans now live in harmony with their environment. Even the Villas at the Wilderness Lodge were supposed to represent the housing for the workers who built the Lodge and the railroad.

In the September 2010 issue of *The Orlando Business Journal*, it was reported that the same area might be developed into a Disney Vacation Club resort with the possibility that the Fort Wilderness Railroad might be revived in some form.

Noah's Ark, Alpine Resort, Typhoon Lagoon The Movie

Noah's Ark

Noah's Ark was announced in a Walt Disney World press release as "the most ambitious nighttime spectacle in Disney Theme Park history" to open in 1992. It would have been staged on the waters of Crescent Lake, primarily for the delight of the upscale guests staying at the Walt Disney World resorts like the Boardwalk and Yacht and Beach Clubs surrounding that body of water. Storyboards were created and models were built. Award-winning composer Andrew Lloyd Webber wrote the score.

Similar to the Electrical Water Pageant, there would be huge floating stages with miles of neon tubing so that the colorful lights could be easily seen.

It was even discussed moving the show to Disney-MGM Studios as the East Coast version of Disneyland's Fantasmic! show. Eventually, it was decided to re-create a version of Fantasmic! for Florida.

Webber also worked on another spectacle show for WDW entitled "EQ" featuring horses that was also never produced. Don Frantz, responsible for producing and directing the Disney World nighttime parade SpectroMagic, managed the conceptual development of both the Webber-proposed shows. Imagineer Eric Jacobson said:

> At the time, we were talking about doing all kinds of different spectaculars. You could say that the basic thinking behind them was one of the keys that led the way to Disney's foray into Broadway.

Alpine Resort

Speaking of water parks, Blizzard Beach was originally going to be connected to a Disney resort. As you now know, Eric Jacobson had a collection of snow globes in his office that inspired the idea of a water park with a winter theme. However, there is more to that story as well.

Located where the Coronado Springs Resort site now stands, Disney's Alpine Resort would have overlooked the melting snows of Blizzard Beach. The Alpine Resort would have been a moderately priced hotel, and as one of the perks for staying there, guests would have been able to ride a chair lift to the water park.

One of the reasons the idea of a hotel connected to a water park was eventually rejected, according to Imagineer Kathy Mangum, was that "the water parks need to be rehabbed just about every year, which means draining them and sandblasting the bottom. We didn't want the guests overlooking an empty water park. It would ruin the story".

Typhoon Lagoon: The Movie

There is an interesting reason why Typhoon Lagoon is the only Disney water park with such an intricately constructed story.

Typhoon Lagoon was designed so that it could be used as a film location for a movie of the same name to be made when that area opened in 1989. According to a Walt Disney World press release, Gary Wolf, the author of the book *Who Censored Roger Rabbit?* (the novel that inspired the film *Who Framed Roger Rabbit*), was writing the screenplay for a film to be called *Typhoon Lagoon*. In fact, Wolf still lists that project on his official resume.

The press release proclaimed that the project was an "unprecedented undertaking whereby a motion picture and a themed attraction...will perfectly complement each other in a unique demonstration of the capabilities of the Walt Disney Company". All of the locations and the Imagineering created characters like Singapore Sal would have sprung to cinematic life.

The Enchanted Snow Palace Ride

Anna, Elsa, and the world of Arendale are coming to the Norway Pavilion at World Showcase. However, decades earlier there was an attempt to create a Magic Kingdom attraction devoted to the story of the Snow Queen.

Walt Disney himself had been interested in the Hans Christian Andersen tale of the Snow Queen as early as 1943.

Walt was in discussions with MGM film producer Samuel Goldwyn to collaborate on a film biography of the famous fairy tale writer. MGM would handle the live-action sequences, and Disney would create short animated sequences of some of Anderson's most famous tales including "The Little Mermaid", "The Steadfast Tin Soldier", and of course, "The Snow Queen".

The project never developed any further, but periodically (just like with the story of the Little Mermaid) the Disney artists would review the material to see if they could develop a story about the Snow Queen.

The big challenge was that the Snow Queen was basically a villain and all of the Disney animated feature films were about heroes who defeated the villain.

In 2002, Disney came close, even having songwriter Alan Menken compose several terrific tunes including "Love Can't Be Denied". Animator Glen Keane was deeply involved in the film, but left when CEO Michael Eisner considered giving the film to Pixar. Fortunately, the project was revived again with a new team in 2008.

A few years before his official retirement in 1978, Marc Davis designed an attraction for Walt Disney World's Fantasyland that was based on the story of the Snow Queen and was entitled the Enchanted Snow Palace.

The massive white-and-blue show building would have looked like a glacier, but as guests got closer and looked more carefully, they would have realized that it seemed almost like carvings of towers, windows, and doors.

Guests would have boarded a boat (just like they do for It's A Small World) to drift pass dancing Audio-Animatronic polar bears, walruses, and penguins, to the background music from "The Nutcracker Suite".

Soon, the guests would drift into a snow cave with frost fairies (like the ones in *Fantasia*) and snow giants carrying icicle clubs. Eventually, the boats would come to the throne room of the Snow Queen herself, who was about to leave on her sled for her journey through her kingdom.

To speed her passage, she conjures up a blizzard and the guests are caught in a brief snow storm flurry just before they exit into the hot summer reality of Fantasyland.

Davis felt that a leisurely, beautiful, air-conditioned attraction that could be enjoyed by guests of all ages would have been embraced by those eager to get out of Florida's heat and humidity and spend a restful moment on a boat ride.

However, at an estimated cost of $15 million, the Disney company decided to pass on the attraction and look to more thrilling rather than artistic experiences.

Epcot is going through a gradual shift away from technology and culture to cartoons and thrills; as a result, in 2016, a similar attraction based on Disney's popular *Frozen* (2013) will debut in the Norway Pavilion.

The new attraction "will take our guests to Arendelle and immerse them in many of their favorite moments and music from the film," said Tom Staggs, chairman of Walt Disney Parks and Resorts. "The broad popularity of *Frozen* will cause even more people to discover and appreciate Norway through a visit to Epcot."

Century 3

On January 9, 1999, the popular Epcot attraction Horizons closed permanently. The creation of Horizons began when the idea for a "space pavilion" was pitched to be part of Epcot Center as early as 1979.

The attraction in Future World was originally going to be called Century 3 (spelled "Century III" on some documents). Just a few years after the U.S. bicentennial in 1976, people were looking forward to the third century in our country's history, and that was the inspiration for the title of the attraction.

However, concerns were brought up that foreign guests wouldn't "get" the implication, so a more universal name needed to be used.

The attraction was temporarily named FutureProbe, which Disney quickly discovered called to mind some type of unpleasant medical procedure or instrument.

The name Horizons was chosen after many discussions between sponsor General Electric and Disney. It implies that we are always striving to reach the horizon, and that when we finally get there, there is another horizon in the distance, and another. The point of the pavilion was to show an achievable future based on existing technology.

Horizons opened exactly one year after Epcot Center opened. Amusingly, the phrase in the attraction—"If we can dream it, we can do it"—that is often falsely credited to Walt Disney was in reality the creation of Imagineer Tom Fitzgerald, who modeled for the Audio-Animatronic "young man" character with the solo submarine.

In 1981, Imagineer Claude Coats talked about the original Century 3 attraction:

> We're going to use a ride device with cars that hang from an overhead rail. It will move 1.8 feet per second. We'll make guests feel they're celebrating the nation's tri-centennial, looking back over the last 100 years.

You will make a two-minute ascent to Future House through thoughts about the future from the past. Then you'll enter a theater for a probe of the future. The screen is more than eight stories high—the biggest screen ever.

It will curve over above the audience to give a planetarium effect. The audience will get views of outer space and inside the molecule. We're taking people to places they've never seen before. Like inside an electron microscope. Into living cells. Out to the rings of Saturn. Along the DNA life chain. There'll be many blowups of microscopic stuff.

It's a celebration of the good times ahead of us. We'll show future urban development. A family celebrating their 100th wedding anniversary, which will be a common thing. We'll show a complete new lifestyle. And robot mining. An undersea habitat. Underground homes. Desert farming. Hobbies, cooking, music as they will be in the future.

We'll end up going into a space habitat. We'll show work and health activity in space. Manufacturing. Mining of minerals from planets or asteroids.

At the end of the experience, we'll tie the whole thing into the family unit.

Still in their ride vehicles, guests would have then left the show and moved into a polling area as the dashboard of their vehicles lit up and they would be prompted to indicate their feelings about what they just saw. The results would be instantly tabulated so guests could compare their reactions against those of others who experienced the attraction.

This is what we might have gotten, but which evolved instead into the Horizons attraction that many Disney fans still miss today.

WDW Time Capsule

Ron Heminger began his Disney career in 1955 as one of the dancers at the Indian village in Frontierland, where his father was a chief. He worked his way up into managerial roles, finishing out his decades with Disney working at Epcot.

Some of his favorite stories were about the building of the Magic Kingdom.

Since Coors beer was only available on the West Coast, and it was a favorite of some of the California people working on the Magic Kingdom in Florida, they arranged for it to be shipped out in boxes from the West Coast marked as equipment for Peter Pan's Flight.

He gathered money from those who wanted a case or two and then arranged to have Disney company trucks bring out the brew in the same shipments as the material being used to build the attractions. Cast member (and later vice-president of the Magic Kingdom) Bill "Sully" Sullivan confirmed:

> Yeah, Ron was right. This guy brought out Coors beer in boxes marked "small tools and parts". He almost got fired because he had used company trucks. Luckily, some of the managers liked Coors, so it was just a warning to stop doing that kind of thing.
>
> Ron was half-Sioux, you know. A bunch of the older guys were offered a buy-out package from Disney and Ron took it and moved out west. He's in a trailer in Arizona somewhere. He was a great guy.

Several years after Magic Kingdom opened in 1971, Heminger was walking with his supervisor through the theme park and reminiscing about the frantic nature of opening the place on time. Some things had to be temporarily covered up or hidden in order to meet the deadline.

Heminger said:

> One of the things I really regret is that we never did the time capsule. We prepared the spot, but just ran out of time.

His supervisor, who was not there in those months of construction, laughed and told him that it was just an urban legend and that there were never any plans for a time capsule. Heminger knew better and insisted that it was true and that a place had been prepared in Cinderella Castle.

The discussion started to escalate, and Heminger finally told the supervisor to meet him at Cinderella Castle a few hours past park closing, after the guests and maintenance staff had left.

When the park closed, Heminger and one of his cohorts went to the Pirates of the Caribbean attraction and took a full skeleton. Then they went to Cinderella Castle and carefully removed a plaque. In the hollowed-out hole behind the plaque, a space had indeed been prepared for something.

They dressed the skeleton in a distinctive WED (Walt Disney Imagineering) hard hat and vest, stuffed it into the opening, and then replaced the plaque.

Later that evening, Heminger met his supervisor at the agreed location and gave him a flashlight. With some theatrical difficulty, Heminger removed the plaque while he told how things were so hectic in the final days of building the Magic Kingdom that they basically spent their energy during the last few days just making sure everything was covered up for the guests until they could get to it again. The same thing had happened just before the opening of Disneyland and some things were never found later.

The supervisor was surprised to see a wide hole hidden behind the plaque. Turning on the flashlight, he curiously stuck his head deep inside and peered below...where he saw the supposed remains of a hapless WED employee inadvertently trapped and forgotten for years.

Fantasia Gardens

Sometimes at Walt Disney World, it will take years for a project to be built, and over the course of those years, it may evolve through many changes.

A Fantasia Gardens was built, but originally it was not meant to be a miniature golf course. In the mid-1960s, Imagineer Marc Davis designed an overlay for Disneyland's Motor Boat Cruise attraction that would have incorporated elements from Disney's *Fantasia* (1940).

Because of the landscaping already in place, as well as Davis' selection of the more bucolic segments from the film, the project was called Fantasia Gardens. Several challenges were unable to be overcome, including Davis' proposal to create "water sculptures" and finding a way to filter the ambient, disruptive noise from the nearby Autopia attraction, so the plans were shelved.

In 1983, with the closing of the beloved Swan Boat ride at the Magic Kingdom in Florida, Imagineer Claude Coats re-examined Davis' plans and came up with a suggestion. He planned to re-theme the water pathway that the Swan Boats took to a *Fantasia* theme and to include new boats that had higher capacity.

Working with Katy Moss Warner of Walt Disney World Parks Horticulture, Coats envisioned topiaries of the *Fantasia* characters along the route.

Coats, along with show producer and writer Mark Eades and vice president of Concept Development Randy Bright, divided the ride into six show scenes, each themed to a sequence of *Fantasia*.

As Eades told me, the first section was going to be a simple, beautiful, colorful garden based on "Toccata in Fugue". There would also be sections devoted to "The Pastoral Symphony", "The Rite of Spring", "The Sorcerer's Apprentice", and two for "Dance of the Hours". "The Sorcerer's Apprentice" section, for instance, would feature giant broomsticks that dumped fountatins of water in the path of the oncoming boats, but miraculously stopped just before the arrival of each boat.

Coats even staged a proof of concept ride-through for Disney executives by taking two water craft from the Seven Seas Lagoon and setting up colorful show cards along the bank. The attraction was estimated to cost approximately $20 million, but no sponsor could be found to fund the project.

Bill "Sully" Sullivan, then the vice-president of the Magic Kingdom, recalled:

> It would have been a beautiful ride. Just beautiful. The pitch and the demonstration went very well. I said I just needed ten minutes with Michael Eisner. I followed Eisner to the bathroom and we were talking and I said, "This is no good to me. I need something with high volume. When it rains, this ride shuts down and I can't use it. I need a bigger bang for my buck." So Eisner comes out and goes to Bright and says, "We need to think through a few more things." And that killed it.

Finally, there were plans to include Fantasia Gardens as part of the Beastly Kingdom section for Disney's Animal Kingdom. The boats would have sailed past Greek architecture, including columns and temples, and Mount Olympus, as well as floated beneath a brightly colored rainbow archway.

According to the Disney press release:

> There is also Fantasia Gardens. A gentle musical boat ride through the animals from Disney's animated classic, *Fantasia*. Both the crocodiles and hippos from "Dance of the Hours" and the Pegasus, fauns, and centaurs from Beethoven's "Pastoral" are found here.

When the Beastly Kingdom area was indefinitely postponed, the concept and the name were repurposed for a miniature golf course near the Walt Disney World Dolphin Resort hotel.

The Disney Family in Florida

In 1878, Kepple Disney and his family, including his two sons Elias (Walt's father) and Robert, left Canada to seek their fortune in California. When Kepple passed through Kansas, he ended up buying a large parcel of land and set up a farm.

During this time, Elias became very fond of Flora Call, the teenaged daughter of a neighbor who lived only two miles from the farm. In 1884, after some very severe winters, the Call family moved to Florida accompanied by Kepple Disney and Elias, who both settled in Acron where there were only seven families at the time.

Kepple was not pleased with Florida and almost immediately moved back to Kansas. Elias bought a forty-acre farm in Kismet. Elias eventually sold the farm to try his hand at managing the Hallifax Hotel in Daytona Beach, but left after the summer tourist season and got a job as a rural mailman in Kissimmee, where he saved enough money to buy an orange grove.

Walt Disney's maternal grandparents were Charles and Henrietta Call, who acquired eighty acres for a farm about a mile north of the settlement.

The Call children were Flora Call (Walt Disney's mother); Jessie Call, who married Albert Perkins in 1887; Grace Lila Call, who married William Frary in 1890; Julia Call, who married Lawrence Campbell in 1897; and Charles Jr. The women became active in the Ladies Society of Kismet, and the family attended church there. Later, they found that they were actually living closer to Acron.

Flora worked as a teacher in Acron for the first year and then in Paisley during her second year. Mr. Call was also a teacher in neighboring Norristown until he died in 1890 after complications from an accident when he was clearing some pine trees.

Walt Disney's parents married in a Lake County ceremony in the Calls' home in Kismet on January 1, 1888. Lake County was formed on May 27, 1887, and issued its first marriage license exactly seven months later for the Disney-Call union. Elias was nearly thirty years old and Flora nineteen. Their first son, Herbert, was born on December 8, 1888.

A frost destroyed Elias' orange crop and he was stricken with malaria, so the Disney family moved back to Chicago in 1889 where Elias found carpentry work building the Columbian Exposition seven days a week at a dollar per day.

Walt Disney's uncle Albert Perkins, who had married his mother's sister Jessie, became the postmaster of Paisley in 1902 and served until 1935.

Jessie taught in several Lake County schools and eventually served as principal of Eustis High School. When her husband died, she succeeded him as postmaster and served until 1946.

The story goes that the young Walt and Roy Disney sometimes visited Jessie and Albert in Florida during their summer vacations from school and fished and hunted in the Ocala National Forest.

Charles was buried in 1890 in Maple Grove Cemetery, located a short distance northeast of Kismet. When his widow, Henrietta, died in 1910, their daughter Jessie had Mr. Call exhumed and buried beside Mrs. Call in Ponceannah Cemetery. They are buried near the back of the cemetery beneath a stone monument that is carved to resemble a tree stump.

Ye Olde Christmas Shoppe in Liberty Square at the Magic Kingdom is meant to represent three separate stores. The section nearest the Liberty Tree restaurant resembles the quaint home of a family of Pennsylvanian German folk artists and craftsmen.

On the outside wall is a blue heart-shaped plaque with the family's name, Kepple. It is an intentional hidden reference to Kepple, Walt's paternal grandfather.

Disney in Disguise

In the beginning of his career, Walt Disney was not a recognized public figure.

Would someone not in the entertainment business instantly recognize Jack Warner or Samuel Goldwyn or Harry Cohn or some other big movie producer? That all changed with the weekly *Disneyland* television show where people saw Uncle Walt encouraging them to come and visit Disneyland.

Walt was now instantly recognizable, and so he tried to disguise himself when he went out in public, sometimes with his hat pulled down to obscure his face.

On one trip, Walt's barber suggested snipping off Walt's mustache. "I don't want to look *that* different" he snorted.

Walt and his older brother Roy used pseudonyms when they physically visited the Florida area before the official announcement was made that Disney was coming. Walt was "Walt Davis" and Roy was "Roy O. Davis". That way they didn't have to change the initials on their luggage or on any other monogrammed items.

If they started to write their names, by the time they got to the "D" they could make the correction. If someone said their first name, they would respond without having to remember they were someone else.

In addition, Imagineer Marvin Davis, who drew the layout for Disneyland and the Magic Kingdom, had married Walt's niece, Marjorie, and he traveled with Walt, so he could legally bring out a driver's license to prove that this was the "Davis" group.

However, there were occasional "close calls" where the ruse might have been revealed.

One night in Orlando, Walt was eating with some associates in a hotel dining room. The waitress kept eyeing him. Finally, she approached and commented, "You know you look a little like Walt Disney."

Walt, so wrapped up in the conversation and now distracted by this remark, replied indignantly, "What do you mean, I *look* like Walt Disney? I *am* Walt Disney!" and he started to pull out his driver's license for proof.

Fortunately, the rest of the group stopped him, said something to the waitress, and the incident never made it to the newspapers. If it had, land prices would have skyrocketed.

Roy would wear dark glasses and a false beard and would claim to be from New York. At a stopover in Miami, he ran into a prominent person he knew and was curious about the effectiveness of his disguise. They had dinner together and it worked, so that the secret was kept.

A window on Main Street in the Magic Kingdom lists the "Pseudonym Real Estate Development Company" and its president, "Roy Davis". Another pseudonym on that window is vice president "Bob Price", the false name used by Bob Price Foster to acquire land for Disney.

Walt and Roy were in Tallahassee (the capital of Florida) on November 14, 1965, and had dinner at the governor's mansion.

Governor William Haydon Burns and the Disney group flew by private plane to Orlando on November 15 and proceeded directly to the Cherry Plaza Hotel where they had a small private luncheon before the press conference officially announcing Disney coming to Florida.

During that visit, Walt toured the WDW site with Joe Fowler, Card Walker, Joe Potter, Roy, Irlo Bronson, and a few others like Bob Foster. It also included a boat tour of Bay Lake and a fried chicken lunch at one of the houses built on the property. He flew back to Burbank a couple days later.

Walt's last trip to the Florida site was for a few days in May 1966.

Getting Hired at Disney World in 1971

Most Disney fans know that people interested in being hired to work at Walt Disney World today generally go to the Casting Building located across the street from Downtown Disney.

Walt Disney World employs approximately 60,000 cast members in a variety of positions and in many different categories.

However, in 1971, before the theme park officially opened for business, the process was different.

In mid-June 1971, Walt Disney World's Employment Department began interviewing applicants for the 5,000 full time jobs that would be available in August and September to prepare for the official October opening of the park.

Those job openings included not just working at the Magic Kingdom, but across the entire property, from the three resorts to the golf courses, watercraft, and many other areas.

Jim Passilla was the director of Employee Relations for Disney's Florida operation. Before the June hiring announcement, a select number of applications were being taken at the Employment Center, on State Route 535, for a "limited number of positions now available".

Passilla stated that Disney interviewers thought of themselves as casting directors for a mammoth entertainment production where there would be no bus boys or waitresses, but rather dining hosts and dining hostesses.

He emphasized that Walt Disney World was a "first-name company", with "no Misters or Sirs", because everyone works together on a first-name basis since "it's friendlier that way". He stated:

> In most cases, we are looking for types of people rather than skills. We do not think of "hiring for a job", but rather of "casting for a role" in the Walt Disney World show.

Passilla pointed out the many different roles available and that all of them were considered important:

> A Custodian Host is the most important public relations man we have because he is apt to get the most questions from guests.
>
> We often hear people refer to clean-cut, attractive, helpful, personable, well-groomed, enthusiastic men and women as "Disney types". These will be the kind of people we will want when we begin interviewing applicants in mid-June.

A press release announced that:

> In looking for cast members to fill the 5,000 Vacation Kingdom roles, the employment staff will be looking primarily for full-time employees since "the show must go on" year round with limited opportunities for part-time employment.

Preference was given to applicants already living in Florida, since it entailed no additional relocation expenses. People were excited to work at the newest Disney theme park and many spent their own money relocating to central Florida in hopes of finding a job working there.

In 1971, for roughly every thirty people who applied for a job, only one was hired. However, cast members used to joke that if you could find the Employment Office, which was hidden away off the beaten track, you would get hired.

Costumes were made in only certain "average" sizes, so applicants who were too tall, too short, or too large were out of luck.

The press release also stated that:

> Dedication to one's role and the company goals offers some opportunity for each cast member, since the company staunchly practices promotion from within. Illustrating that fact is Dick Nunis, Vice President of Operations at both Disneyland in California and Walt Disney World, who began with Disneyland as a departmental clerk sixteen years ago.

Since those days decades ago, the hiring process and orientation have changed significantly.

Disney World's First Costumed Mickey Mouse

Doug Parks was born in Auburn, New York, on August 15, 1950, to Dawse and Margaret Parks. He attended Weedsport Central High School and graduated in 1969. He had two older brothers, Ralph and Lowrey.

The red-headed Parks was a high school track star in upstate New York and known for his agility and cheerfulness.

In April 1971, Parks moved to his brother's house in central Florida so he could apply for work at Walt Disney World, which was due to open in six months. He was roughly four foot eight (today, the height range for Mickey is usually between four foot ten and five foot two) and never weighed more than 95 pounds in his life.

"He was a little fellow," his brother Ralph Parks recalled in a 2010 interview, but "he had a giant personality."

A story and picture of Parks that ran in a 1971 issue of *The Orlando Sentinel* identified him as the first Mickey Mouse. He trained two "substitute" East Coast mice for the earliest days of Walt Disney World.

As a "friend" of Mickey, he traveled around the country as well as Canada and South America promoting the newest Disney theme park. However, his most memorable and important moment was the dedication of Walt Disney World where Roy O. Disney motioned for him to join him as Roy read his speech.

John Hench recounted:

> Roy Disney stood facing the microphone before a crowd of guests ready to deliver the dedication speech at the opening ceremony. He suddenly turned and looked around and I heard him say quietly, "Somebody go find Mickey for me. We don't have Walt any more, and Mickey is the nearest thing to Walt that we have left." Mickey appeared and Roy promptly began his speech, with Mickey standing proudly at his side.

Actually, looking at photos of the occasion, Mickey is respectfully bowing his head with his hands folded in front of him, completely aware of the importance of the occasion and the significance of his presence at that moment in time.

Parks did collect Disney memorabilia and was a strong Disney fan and supporter for his entire life. Some cast members and friends knew him for his sense of humor and his joking phrases "that's all rat" or "you will always be all rat" or just plain "all rat".

During his 39 years with Disney, he moved on to other roles, including the mailroom. At one time, he was a sort of "secret shopper" sent to visit the WDW resort hotels and write reports. Toward the end of his career he worked at the Disney Reservation Center, making reservations and helping schedule trips for guests.

When Parks passed away from cancer on August 29, 2010, at 8 a.m., two weeks after his 60th birthday, the Disney company would not admit that Parks was the first Mickey Mouse, to avoid spoiling the magic as well as the headline that Mickey Mouse was dead, but did confirm he was an Entertainment cast member in the early 1970s.

Walt Disney World Resort President Meg Crofton wrote in a letter to Parks' family:

> For four decades, Walt Disney World was a better place thanks to Doug and his contributions. He was an important part of our business of making dreams come true.

"Often they would refer to Douglas as the mayor of Disney," remembered Ralph Parks.

Doug Parks, according to his wishes, was cremated, but the magical memories he created, especially as the first East Coast Mickey, will never die and are still an inspiration to others who perform as Mickey today.

Getting the Park Open on Deadline

As former Chairman of Walt Disney Attractions Dick Nunis recalled:

> Card Walker and Donn Tatum called me into the office on Monday morning in late May 1971 and said, "If we turn the total energies of the company in one direction, Dick, would you be willing to go down and get it open on deadline?" There was no time to worry about budgets. They told me I could get anyone and anything I called for. There was no discussion of changing the date.
>
> I carried a tape recorder and dictated all day long as I went around the project. Secretaries typed the memos at night and sent them out the next day.

Ron Miziker, who was one of the people in charge of entertainment, remembered:

> Does anyone mention the Nunis Death Marches? He'd take the top people in each division and walk them through the park during the day, pointing out stuff and asking why things weren't done.

Former Vice-President of Disney World Bob Allen talked about the infamous managers' meetings that Nunis would call:

> They kept getting earlier and earlier. Finally, we got word to be in the meeting room at 6 a.m. There were some phone calls among us and when Dick walked in next morning we were all there in our pajamas. Jack Olsen [director of merchandising] had a mug and was shaving himself. Dick got the idea and after that he held the meetings at 7 a.m.

Nunis said:

> The turning point was Labor Day. We couldn't get the construction crews to work that day. We decided if they wouldn't work, we would. We would show them what it's all about. We opened up the theme park and all of us turned out to man the attractions. We invited the construction workers to come out with their families and enjoy the day on us.
>
> We had 10,000–12,000 people Kids would say to their daddies, "Daddy, did you really build that?" It gave the men a feeling of importance.

And it worked. We told them afterward, "Help us, guys, and we'll have your families back again." And you know, it was amazing the amount of work we got done the rest of that week.

On Thursday, September 30, 1971, the Contemporary Resort looked austere as it rose above the empty landscape. There was no grass, no bushes or trees to be seen. Dick Nunis took charge and shortly before 5 p.m., about fifteen hours before the Magic Kingdom would open to guests for the first time, Nunis began directing like a general a ragtag troop of college students, cast members, and some unskilled workers.

Disney landscaper Bill Evans recalled:

> Planting a few palm trees would be no problem, but we also figured it would take about four-and-a-half acres of sod just to make the place look presentable. Given the timetable, most everyone thought it an impossible task. Everyone but Nunis. He made the calls to have the sod trucked in, hired about a hundred extra men, none of whom knew anything about laying sod, grabbed anybody else that was standing around, and began turning the brown earth green.

It grew dark as the precious hours ticked by and the workers lugged heavy clumps of grass across the vast expanse. However, for decades, the one thing that people remembered about that night was Nunis in a loud and hoarse voice proclaiming, "Green side up! Remember, green side up!"

By 6 a.m. the next morning, the Contemporary was ready for the guests and the Magic Kingdom opened on time.

The Life Magazine Photo

Most Walt Disney World fans would not recognize the name of Bill Spidle, but for fourteen years (beginning in 1969) he was the photographer at Walt Disney World. One of his memories of that time period was the photo that graced the cover of the October 15, 1971, issue of *Life* magazine. He said:

> *Life* editors called and wanted to do a cover, showing the Magic Kingdom castle. Posed in front of the castle would be a cast of thousands. This was quickly negotiated down to a cast of a hundred or so.

> A *Life* cover was considered something of a big deal, and even though this was mid-August, and people were busy as hell doing a hundred things, all on deadline, everybody in the Magic Kingdom sort of switched from worker to spectator the minute the *Life* team arrived. With the October opening right on his shoulder, this was just the thing that drove Dick Nunis crazy.

> They decided they'd roll out the complete cast of Magic Kingdom characters…in full costume. Then they added all the ride attendants, guides, cooks, clean-up crews, musicians, assorted Disney brass, and got them set up with the castle in the background.

> It was a typical August day, about 96.3 in the shade—and no shade. The photographer, Yale Joel, set up lights, equipment, and himself on two cherry-pickers and started running tests. An hour went by. Several people fainted. New people had to be costumed and positioned.

> It's bright sunlight out and I can't figure what he's testing, but I'm not a *Life* photographer, right? Anyway, he's testing this and that, and in the process testing the hell out of Nunis. He's going absolutely nuts. People are just standing around! Time is being wasted!

> Me? I'm having a good time taking pictures. I looked up at one point and realized I had shot six rolls of 35mm—and the *Life* photographer is still testing. I know he's only going to be perfect, but I don't think Nunis is going to survive. After three or four hours of testing, he got off that one shot. I'll have to admit it was a helluva picture.

The magazine included a seven-page article with lots of color photos entitled "Mickey Opens in Florida: Disney Goes East", which read in part:

> The new site is Florida, but the air is pure old Disney. Who else could be responsible for this carefully crafted vision of the American past, the intricate, hokey, hugely expensive assemblage of lives and places that never were? Walt Disney World, which opened this month is $400 million worth of amusement park, vacation resort, and planned model city enameled onto the scrub-pine flats outside Orlando, Florida. The Disney trademark is all over it: the businesslike use of fantasy, the no-nonsense approach to nonsense.
>
> Disney World incorporates some lessons learned in the original gold mine called Disneyland that opened sixteen years ago in Anaheim, California. Some changes are minor. At Orlando, the vinyl leaves on the Swiss Family Robinson Tree are draped with live Spanish moss. No such decoration at Anaheim.
>
> The biggest lesson Disney's people learned in Anaheim was on the periphery of the park, where a jungle of independent restaurants, hotels, and other amusements moved in. "At Anaheim," says a Disney officer, "we lost control of the environment." They also lost control of an estimated $500 million business created by Disney's draw. For these and other reasons, where Disneyland is just over 200 acres, Disney World is gigantic: 27,400 acres. Control of the environment and the moneymaking is not likely to escape again.

Disney World's First Ambassador, Debbie Dane

In December 1969, Debbie Dane (now Brown, and a mother) was 18 years old when she heard that Walt Disney World was looking for fourteen hostesses for their new Preview Center.

She was among the first hired and spent her days explaining to curious tourists what Walt Disney World would be like when it opened, because there were many misconceptions. She was born and raised in Forest City, Florida.

In 1970, she became the first Walt Disney World Ambassador, and as part of her responsibilities she took people out to the construction site and gave tours. She would point to balloons hovering over the property and explain what was going to be built in that particular location.

Her term lasted a few months longer than the normal year for Disney park ambassadors so that she could participate in the opening month activities. Dane recalled:

> It was almost like the place was a child and I was watching it grow. I began to feel a part of it in many ways. I remember driving across Bay Lake after they had drained it and parking for a while right at the middle. Now I go back and point it out to my kids and tell them how I once parked there.

Dane was one of the many cast members who helped lay sod at the Contemporary the night before opening day, though she left early to spend the night with her parents at their Forest City home so that she would be fresh and sharp in the morning. However, Debbie remembered that neither she nor her parents seemed to get much sleep:

> All three of us woke about three in the morning. Nobody could get back to sleep, so everyone piled into the car and we headed for the Polynesian Hotel, where I was scheduled to report at five. Near the

park entrance, traffic was incredible. I later learned these were people who had spent the night cruising back and forth on I-4, jockeying to be the first family at the ticket gate. We finally had to call Security to escort us to the hotel.

We fussed around, getting ready for the big moment. Just the anticipation was a delicious kind of crazy. Nobody knew how it would be. I was filled with every kind of emotion. Walking near Cinderella Castle, I watched all the Big Guys [company executives] watching the entrances. You knew they were probably as nervous as anyone. Finally, the gates opened and Mickey and I went to meet the family being honored as Disney World's first guests.

They had this cute little boy. He was about two years old. Mickey and I each grabbed a hand and started him on the tour. He was just overwhelmed, of course. At one point he looked up at me wide-eyed and said, "This is better than Christmas!" I haven't heard anything in all these years that can match that in describing Disney World.

That night, Dane attended a celebration at the Polynesian Village Resort, as remembered by Edward Prizer, then the editor of *Orlando Magazine*:

I brought my wife Artice out to the Polynesian for dinner in the glittering new Papeete Bay dining room. The room was filled with handsomely dressed Disney officials, the people who had created all this, relaxing for the first time in years.

Tahitian drums throbbed and Polynesian dancers undulated under the spotlight on stage. Champagne corks popped. New crystal and silver sparkled. Looking out the broad windows, through the palms and torches across the lagoon, we gazed at the gem-like radiance of Cinderella Castle in the distance. Was it even now just all a dream?

Bob Hope at Disney World

Comedian Bob Hope was a guest on NBC's *The Grand Opening of Walt Disney World*, which aired on October 29, 1971. He entered the Contemporary Hotel via monorail and launched into his monologue:

> It's really two buildings leaning against each other. And I want to congratulate the architect...Dean Martin. I have a lovely room with complete privacy, except in the bathtub which Donald Duck shares with me. Have you ever tried bathing with a duck who was playing with his rubber man?

> I ordered lunch from room service. Snow White brought it in and I was afraid to eat the apple. I don't dare drink the water because that was delivered by Pluto.

> This is the biggest vacation-entertainment complex in the world. And to think it all started with a gentle mouse, a bad-tempered duck, and seven mixed-up dwarfs. It's a fantastic achievement. They took a swamp and turned it into a Magic Kingdom. It wasn't easy. Have you ever tried to relocate 8,000 angry alligators?

> Walt Disney always believed in the beauty and natural wonders of the world. But he felt as we passed through that we should try to add a little wonder and beauty to it. Maybe you'll understand that Walt's dream was just a beginning. The dream doesn't stop here. This is the start of it. I think you'll want to tell your grandchildren you were there when it happened.

Near the end of the program, Hope returned with an even more moving tribute:

> Walt Disney World is the culmination of a lifetime devoted to bringing joy and excitement and laughter to children and adults in America and throughout the world. There is a spirit here everywhere. All of this is Walt.

> This is what Walt wanted for all of us...an escape from our aspirin existence into a land of sparkles and lights and rainbows. Walt Disney loved America. He loved its children and their moms and pops. Walt

Disney loved America because his dreams came true. The entire world owes Walt a great debt. He achieved much, but perhaps his greatest accomplishment is that he made children of us all.

Tom Nabbe, who was in charge of the monorails during the opening of Walt Disney World, recalled:

> For the filming of the opening special, we drove Bob Hope into the Contemporary Hotel concourse on the monorail to do his bit. I was standing on the platform waiting for him when one of the coordinators came up to me. These were the days when the monorails had individual air conditioners in them and they made quite a noise.
>
> So this guy says, "Tom, the noise is drowning out Bob's monologue. Can you do something about it?" And I went over and hit the power button. Then I picked up the phone and called the monorail roundhouse and said, "You'd better get over here because we've got to haul Bob Hope out of this building in fifteen minutes and you need to re-set the rectifiers because I just turned them off."
>
> And they got over and were standing by so that the minute Hope finished they could re-set the rectifiers. The only way I could shut off the air conditioning units on the train was to kill the power to the train, which I did. Then I had to get it started back up so we could take Hope on his merry way back to the Polynesian.

The Bwana Bob merchandise cart at the entrance of Adventureland was named in honor of Bob Hope's 1963 comedy film *Call Me Bwana*.

Disney World's First Christmas 1971

An announcement in the December 12, 1971 edition of *The Orlando Sentinel* newspaper stated:

> Walt Disney World's first Christmas will be a spirited two-week holiday full of gaiety, tradition, colorful Disney character parades, and commemorative religious pageantry of the season. Yuletide decorations will bring added sparkle to the already fun-filled Magic Kingdom—"decked out" literally for Christmas with a giant tree and hundreds of wreaths of hemlock and holly. Special daily Holiday Parades and two mammoth candlelight processionals are part of the spectacular events scheduled for the holidays.
>
> Florally adorned by poinsettias, snapdragons, petunias, and 50,000 pansies, the theme park will feature lights and decorations in each of the Main Street shop windows. And in Town Square, a snowy, 50-foot Christmas tree, especially selected and cut from a forest in Paradise, Michigan, will serve as a colorful centerpiece for the festive theme park celebration. More than 1,200 lights and a thousand giant ornaments adorn the tree.

The Christmas Parade was very similar to the one staged at Disneyland for many years and featured the marching toy soldiers and dancing reindeer that had been designed by Disney artist Bill Justice. Those seasonal characters delighted audiences for decades. Of course, the grand finale was the appearance of jolly Santa Claus himself.

When the tradition of the Candlelight Processional was transplanted to Florida in 1971, Dr. Charles Hirt helped shepherd the original Walt Disney World version. Hirt, then chairman of the Choral Music Department at the University of Southern California, was the man responsible for creating Disneyland's original Candlelight Processional in 1958 and supervising it for years.

Over time there have been variances in the narration script and some different musical selections between the two parks, but the core of the ceremony has basically remained the same.

Walt Disney World's first Candlelight Processional was only held on two nights, December 18 and 19, 1971, at 6 p.m. The nearly 1,200 carolers from across the state of Florida walked down Main Street to the Cinderella Castle forecourt where the performance took place, since most of the early Magic Kingdom shows were staged in that natural hollow space between the two sloping walkways that led up to the castle.

Actor Rock Hudson narrated the Christmas story while Frederick Fennell conducted the orchestra. The living Christmas tree was made up of boys' choirs from Orlando and St. Petersburg. Hudson would eventually perform the narrator role six times in Florida and three in California.

The selection of Hudson was interesting because he did not make a positive impact on Magic Kingdom guests during the three-day dedication ceremony earlier in October. According to a news report in *The Orlando Sentinel*, Hudson "disappointed many female fans over the weekend by refusing to sign autographs or have his picture taken" and physically trying to hide when fans approached.

On the other hand, other celebrities at the event like Cesar Romero, Annette Funicello, Fess Parker, Robert Stack, and Sebastian Cabot had been exceedingly gracious and welcoming to their many raucous fans.

The Magic Kingdom was open on Christmas Eve from 9 a.m. to 6 p.m. Christmas Day hours were 10 a.m. to 6 p.m. Extended hours of 9 a.m. to midnight were in effect for the week between Christmas and New Year's. The park remained open until 2 a.m. on New Year's Eve as part of the first Walt Disney World New Year's Party.

Winnie the Pooh for President Press Event 1972

Winnie the Pooh ran for president at both Disneyland and Walt Disney World in three different election years: 1968, 1972, and finally 1976. He lost every single time by a wide margin, which may account for him never running again.

Pooh was nominated to run for president on the Children's Party Ticket at a convention event on October 1, 1972. Thanks to the connection with Sears, Roebuck and Co. stores who were to support this new promotion, delegates to the convention (and their families) had been selected by Sears in each of the fifty states to be sent to WDW.

Pooh was nominated by popular acclaim in the forecourt of Cinderella Castle. His press secretary was Tigger, his political advisor was Eeyore, and his running mate was Owl who "appealed to both left and right wingers".

Among Pooh's ever changing policy promises was hunny in every pot, licking the high price of ice cream cones, and banning spankings.

Edward Prizer left his job at the Associated Press in New York. He saw that Orlando was on the verge of growth and, in 1962, he purchased for $17,000 a small, pocket-sized tourist guide (restaurants, churches, area attractions like Gatorland) with a readership of 1,700 called the *Orlando-Winter Park Attraction*.

He ran the publication from his home with his wife, Artice, and shifted the content to more news about the area development. His wife hated trivia and wanted substantial stories. The magazine quickly evolved to include lengthy feature stories, real estate news, tourist news, business news, and development issues like the impact of Disney coming to Orlando.

Prizer changed the name of the magazine to *Orlando-Land* in 1969 and sold it in 1988 for $1.7 million with more than 30,000 dedicated readers. He remained as an adviser and wrote a column titled "Inside Orlando" for eight years until he officially retired in 1996.

He died at the age of 80 in 2003, roughly a year and a half after the death of his wife.

Prizer was the primary source for information about Walt Disney World for decades. He attended all the events and interviewed most of the key Disney people. Here are his memories of the 1972 press event for the "Pooh for President" campaign:

> There was a big political rally on a Saturday afternoon in the open field beyond Frontierland. We disemarked from the train at the new Frontierland railroad staion. The rostrum is draped in red, white, and blue bunting. A band plays old-time tunes.
>
> For each of us [in the press], a picnic box stuffed with fried chicken, ham sandwiches, pickles, and such. The smiling hosts pin us with "Pooh for President" buttons and cap us with straw hats bearing "Pooh for President" streamers.
>
> Each of us receives a handful of wooden nickels. They prove to be legal tender for the day, good for Pepsis, corn on the cob, and watermelon. They never did it up so good for William Jennings Bryan.
>
> We cheer the speeches, shake hands with the candidate, dance to the Dixieland band, and afterwards have the run of the Magic Kingdom until midnight.
>
> If we hadn't learned it already, we were now fully cognizant of Disney's way of doing even the simplest things. It's not the thing in itself that counts so much as the aura they surround it with. The theme that lifts it out of the ordinary. The play-acting sweeps you away, however you may resist it. It is always and everywhere, even at a press party, and only when you understand it can you understand the way this organization thinks and functions.

The Only Magic Kingdom Comic Book

Western Printing and Lithographing was the parent company of Whitman Publishing and Simon & Schuster, Inc., and had the exclusive book rights to all the Walt Disney characters beginning in 1933.

Over the decades they used these characters in coloring books, sticker books, storybooks, Little Golden Books, games, puzzles, and other publications, including comic books released through Dell Publishing from 1940–1962, when Western took over producing their own comic book line and called it Gold Key.

Western Publishing didn't hesitate to invest $200,000 in Disneyland, Inc., an investment which bought them 13.8% of Walt's new theme park in 1954.

Between 1955 and 1960, Dell produced ten special Disneyland Giant comic books containing nearly a thousand pages of new, original content of Mickey Mouse and the gang visiting the Happiest Place on Earth.

When the Disney company bought back Western's shares in Disneyland, the publisher continued to produce the regular, profitable Disney comic books, but there seemed to be less urgency to create any more comic book stories about Disneyland to help support Western's investment in the park.

In the late 1960s, comic books (because of their small profit to retailers compared with magazines) were having difficulties finding distribution outlets. Gold Key tried several different formats, including oversized comics, three comics bundled in a plastic bag, square-bound paperback comic book collections, and the digest format.

The digest format had proven a gold mine for Archie Publications, since the smaller size could be displayed near the checkout cash register at supermarkets like issues of *TV Guide* for an impulse purchase and, primarily, the contents relied on reprinted material, saving on production costs.

Walt Disney Comics Digest was published for 57 issues from 1968–1976. The contents consisted (with few exceptions) mainly of reprints from the various previously published Disney comics. In the beginning, the issues were about 192 pages long.

Walt Disney World fans should be on the lookout for issue number 32, dated December 1971 although it was available in October. It is the only comic book that has the Disney characters exploring the newly opened Magic Kingdom in Florida.

For the reprinted stories (re-using a Fantasyland story from a previous comic, for instance), a new opening splash page was drawn by Disney comics artist Tony Strobl, with the realistic backgrounds most likely done by artist Dan Spiegle, who drew some of the more realistic live-action Disney comic book adaptations.

The book is filled with new and reprinted game pages and puzzles as well. However, there were two original stories. One featured Scrooge McDuck going back to the Main Street of his youth drawn by Disney comics artist Pete Alvarado.

Alvarado also drew a nineteen-page Frontierland story where Mickey Mouse and Donald Duck go to enjoy the Country Bear Jamboree except three of the bears (Ernest, Big Al, and Teddi Barra) have disappeared and must be found for the show to go on. This is the only comic book appearance of these Audio-Animatronic characters.

In 1985, young visitors to Epcot got a complimentary copy of a 16-page full-color comic book entitled *Mickey Mouse and Goofy Explore the Universe of Energy at Epcot*, with art by Tony Strobl and written by Carl Fallberg.

It was produced by the Walt Disney Educational Media Company in conjunction with Exxon, the sponsor of the Universe of Energy Pavilion in Future World. It was not for sale on regular newsstands. The comic emphasized that while there are other alternative sources of energy, none of them can beat the fossil fuels that Exxon was providing at such low cost.

About the Author

Jim Korkis is an internationally respected Disney historian who has written hundreds of articles about all things Disney for over three decades. He is also an award-winning teacher, professional actor and magician, and author of several books.

Jim grew up in Glendale, California, right next to Burbank, the home of the Disney studio.

As a teenager, Jim got a chance to meet Disney animators and Imagineers who lived nearby and began writing about them for local newspapers. Over the decades, Jim pursued a teaching career as well as a performing career, but was still active in writing about Disney for various magazines.

In 1995, he relocated to Orlando, Florida, to take care of his ailing parents. He got a job doing magic and making balloon animals for guests at Pleasure Island. Within a month, he was moved over to the Magic Kingdom, where he "assisted in the portrayal of" Prospector Pat in Frontierland as well as Merlin the Magician in Fantasyland for the Sword in the Stone ceremony.

In 1996, he became a full-time salaried animation instructor at the Disney Institute where he taught every animation class, including several that only he taught. He also instructed classes on animation history and improvisational acting techniques for the interns at Disney Feature Animation Florida. As the Disney Institute re-organized, Jim joined Disney Adult Discoveries, the group that researched, wrote, and facilitated backstage tours and programs for Disney guests and Disneyana conventions.

Eventually, Jim moved to Epcot where he was a coordinator with College and International Programs and then a coordinator for the Epcot Disney Learning Center. During his time at Epcot, Jim researched, wrote, and facilitated over two hundred different presentations on Disney history for Disney cast members and Disney's corporate clients including Feld Entertainment, Kodak, Blue Cross, Toys "R" Us, and Military Sales.

Jim was the off-camera announcer for the syndicated television series *Secrets of the Animal Kingdom*; wrote articles for Disney publications like *Disney Adventures*, *Disney Files* (DVC), *Sketches*, and *Disney Insider*. He worked on special projects like writing text for WDW trading cards, as the on-camera host for the 100 Years of Magic Vacation planning video, as facilitator with the Disney Crew puppet show, and countless other credits, such as assisting Disney Cruise Line, WDW Travel Company, Imagineering, and Disney Design Group with Disney historical material. As a result, Jim was the recipient of the prestigious Disney award, Partners in Excellence, in 2004. (Jim is not currently an employee of the Disney Company.)

Several websites feature Jim's essays about Disney history:

- MousePlanet.com
- AllEars.net
- Yesterland.com
- CartoonResearch.com
- WDWRadio.com
- YourFirstVisit.net

To read more stories by Jim Korkis about Disney history, please purchase his other books, all available from Theme Park Press (ThemeParkPress.com).

More Books from Theme Park Press

Theme Park Press publishes dozens of books each year for Disney fans and for general and academic audiences. Here are just a few of our titles. For the complete catalog, including book descriptions and excerpts, please visit:

ThemeParkPress.com

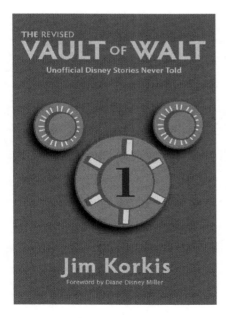

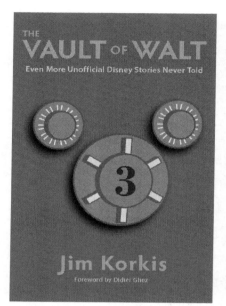

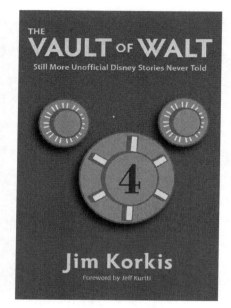

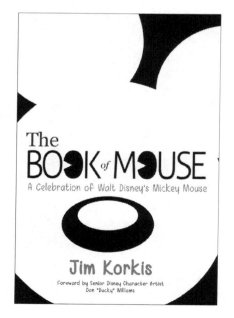

Who's the Leader of the Club?
Walt Disney's Leadership Lessons

JIM KORKIS

Foreword by Henry Hardt
Professor of Business Law and Professor of Finance
Buena Vista University

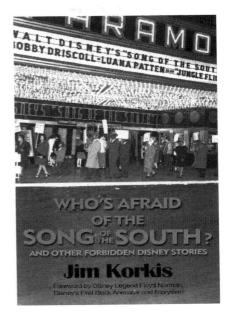

WALT DISNEY'S "SONG OF THE SOUT
BOBBY DRISCOLL-LUANA PATTEN and "JUNGLE FLI

WHO'S AFRAID
OF THE
SONG OF THE SOUTH?
AND OTHER FORBIDDEN DISNEY STORIES

Jim Korkis

Foreword by Disney Legend Floyd Norman,
Disney's First Black Animator and Storyman

From Disneyland's
Tom Sawyer
to Disney Legend

The Adventures of Tom Nabbe

TOM NABBE

From
Jungle Cruise Skipper
to Disney Legend

40 Years of Magical Memories at Disney

William "Sully" Sullivan

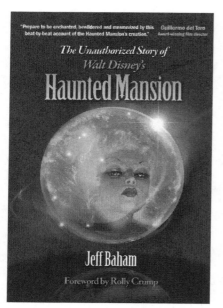

Made in the USA
Lexington, KY
12 October 2017